2.71

THE
PSALMS

The Bible Reading Fellowship
15 The Chambers, Vineyard
Abingdon OX14 3FE
brf.org.uk

The Bible Reading Fellowship (BRF) is a Registered Charity (233280)

ISBN 978 1 84101 648 1
First published 2014
Reprinted 2018
10 9 8 7 6 5 4 3 2 1
All rights reserved

Acknowledgements
Unless otherwise stated, quotations from the Psalms are taken from *Revised Grail Psalms* copyright © 2008, Conception Abbey/The Grail, admin. by GIA Publications, Inc., www.giamusic.com. All rights reserved.

Unless otherwise stated, other biblical quotations are taken from The New Jerusalem Bible, published and copyright © 1985 by Darton, Longman and Todd Ltd and les Editions du Cerf, and by Image Books, a division of Random House, Inc. Used by permission of Darton, Longman and Todd Ltd, and Image Books, a division of Random House, Inc.

The New Revised Standard Version of the Bible, Anglicised edition, copyright © 1989, 1995 by the Division of Christian Education of the National Council of the Churches of Christ in the United States of America, and are used by permission. All rights reserved.

The Jerusalem Bible © 1966 by Darton, Longman and Todd Ltd, and Image Books, a division of Random House, Inc.

A catalogue record for this book is available from the British Library

Printed and bound by CPI Group (UK) Ltd, Croydon CR0 4YY

THE
PSALMS

A COMMENTARY
FOR PRAYER AND REFLECTION

HENRY WANSBROUGH

These reflections on the Psalms were originally published by the Bible Reading Fellowship, twelve psalms at a time, over the period 2010–2014. I am grateful to Jeremy Duff for the invitation to write them, and to Lisa Cherrett for many helpful suggestions in the course of her careful editing.

Contents

Introduction

The Psalter is Israel's prayer book but also the prayer book of the Church. Ancient tradition attributes authorship of the psalms to King David, a tradition that reflects the memorable story of young David playing the harp to soothe King Saul, and also reverence for David as founder of the temple liturgy. We do not know how the psalms were collected, how they were selected or how they were preserved – presumably in the temple. We know that some of them, like Psalm 112[113], were used in the celebration of family festivals, but of their wider liturgical use we know nothing. The Psalms of Ascent were presumably used by pilgrims going up to Jerusalem. Some of the psalms themselves suggest a refrain to be sung in response; some presuppose instruments, the clash of cymbals or a fanfare of trumpets. Some celebrate a public victory or lament a national defeat. But what of the more private psalms? Was there a store of them on which the worshipper could draw at request?

Like other collections of religious poetry, the Psalms express many moods, reflect on many situations and fit many different occasions. They cover, then, the whole sweep of Israel's history and spirituality. Some are based on ancient Canaanite hymns, still retaining traces of the pre-Israelite religion of Canaan – hymns to the god of storm, thunder and lightning (Psalm 28[29]). Others reflect the triumphs and glory of the monarchy in Jerusalem (Psalms 43[44] and 109[110]). Still others sing of the sadness of exile in Babylon, when the nation was carried off to captivity and servitude, leaving Jerusalem and its temple in ruins (Psalm 136[137]). It was during this period of exile that observance of the Law became the dominant feature of Judaism, so the psalms of this period are characterised by love of the Law (Psalms 1 and 118[119]) and by the repentance for sin which was so evident in the spirituality of the exile (Psalm 50[51]). Still other psalms, especially the Psalms of Ascent (Psalms 119—133[120—134]) may sing of the joy of returning to Jerusalem on pilgrimage for the great festivals. There are psalms of national victory and psalms of national defeat, psalms of individual achievement and psalms of individual failure, psalms that hymn the work of God in nature and psalms that celebrate the work of God in the history of Israel. Some psalms beg for release from trials; others thank God for deliverance.

By praying the psalms, we enter into the process of the gradual revelation to Israel, meeting God through the rough and sometimes primitive notions of early Israel, and seeing at the same time the hints of a fuller revelation which was to come in Jesus Christ. The expression of this fuller truth often uses the language of the earlier scripture, giving it a new meaning and a new light.

More than this, the psalms were the prayers of Mary and Jesus: Mary's Magnificat is shot through with reminiscences of the psalms, and Jesus is shown in three of the gospels as dying with a psalm-prayer on his lips. As early as Peter's speech at Pentecost, the psalms began to be used (often stretching their original sense a little) to explain and comment on the resurrection and exaltation of Jesus. This fuller, Christian sense of the psalms is part of the treasury and prayer of the Church.

Three technicalities

Translation

The original language of the psalms is Hebrew. Now Hebrew is a craggy and succinct language. Especially in poetry, each word is pregnant with sense and allusion. The eight Hebrew words of Psalm 19[20]:7 are rendered by 28 in English. This can give the impression of a series of uncoordinated hammer-blows of sense or imagery. The Hebrew was translated into Greek a century or two before Christ. This version is called the Septuagint because, according to legend, it was produced by 70 translators. It often differs widely from the Hebrew text that we now have, and may represent a Hebrew version earlier than and different from what we now possess. In any case, English versions of the psalms often differ considerably as the translator struggles to express the sense and implications of the words. The translator must also decide whether to reproduce the 'cragginess' of the poetry (similar to the English poetry of Gerard Manley Hopkins and T.S. Eliot) or whether to offer a smoother and more flowing English text. Myles Coverdale's version, used in the Anglican Book of Common Prayer, is mellifluous and polished. In the New Jerusalem Bible, I tried to remain closer to the craggy and suggestive nature of the original Hebrew.

A note on numbering

The numbering of the psalms given here follows the Greek version. The Hebrew text divides the Greek Psalm 9 into two (9 and 10), and thus stays one ahead until Psalm 148. The Roman Catholic tradition follows the Greek numbering, but many Protestant versions adopt the Hebrew numbering, following Luther's preference for the Hebrew. When using a Protestant version (such as NRSV or NIV), add 1 to all psalm references between 9 and 148.

The 'titles' of the psalms

Often, at the beginning of a psalm, a short phrase is given (in some editions printed in italics), which is not an original part of the psalm but (in the Greek text used for this book) constitutes 'verse 1' of the psalm. Where this is the case, the verse numbering will remain one ahead of the Hebrew version throughout. In this commentary, a reminder is given each time the psalm in question has a title as verse 1.

The titles are sometimes 'stage directions', naming the composer or the choir for which it was intended, or the instruments or the tune to be used. Many of them, on the assumption that the psalms were written by David, attempt to fit the psalm into a particular situation in David's life. These titles are very old but are not part of the original psalm and do not have full biblical authority.

How to use this book

These meditations were written as daily reflection on the psalms. One possible way of using them has three elements: it follows the traditional monastic method of *lectio divina*, or prayerful reading, outlined by Guigo II, Prior of the Grande Chartreuse in 1170:

- First read the psalm slowly, carefully and thoughtfully, aware that God is speaking to you through it. Guigo likens this to rolling a grape around on the tongue.
- Then read the reflection, referring to the psalm to see what light the reflection throws on the psalm – whether what it says is true and helpful. This is a sort of studious reading. Perhaps look up any cross-reference given in your Bible. For Guigo, this is the prolonged chewing of the grape.
- Return to the psalm itself in prayer. What message has the Lord for you in this? In the first place it was not written for you, but it still has a message for you. Here is received the full flavour of the grape.
- Allow the tranquillity of God to flow over you and fill you with peace.

Book 1

Psalm 1: Blessed indeed is the man

This psalm is carefully placed at the beginning of the Psalter. It is a Wisdom psalm. A great deal of the Wisdom literature at the end of the Old Testament period gives rules and hints about how to get on in life. Much of the advice is in the form of wise proverbs, not always particularly religious: 'Bread is sweet when it is won by fraud, but later the mouth is full of grit' (Proverbs 20:17). However, through it all runs the thread that all wisdom comes from the Lord.

Sorting the psalms into categories sometimes contributes to easier understanding. Several of the psalms fall into this category of celebrating the blessing on those who set themselves to fulfil God's Law. Such psalms often begin, 'Blessed are those who...' (for example, Psalms 31[32], 40[41], 111[112] and 127[128]). Two of the special Wisdom psalms are our present psalm and the lengthy Psalm 118[119]. It has been suggested that they were placed at the beginning and end of a primitive collection of psalms as a sort of inclusive literary bracket, thus stressing the importance of observing the Law for all prayer and service.

These psalms of the Law are joyful psalms, for obedience to the Law is a joyful response in love to a gift in love. The Law is no burden but a pleasure and privilege. It is God's set of instructions on how to remain close to God, given to his own special people. It is both a gift in friendship and a revelation of God's own nature. Obedience to the Law is a matter of imitation of God: 'Be holy as I am holy' is the theme song of the Law in Leviticus. Obedience is not a way of earning salvation but is a loving response to a gift made in friendship. This is what makes it so full of joy.

This little psalm conceals its artistry. First comes the blessing on those who stand apart from sinners and delight in the Law. Then there is an image for this blessing – the tree planted beside flowing waters. In a dry land, water is the secret of life, and not every tree flourishes. I think especially of a particular tree, growing luxuriously beside the sparkling stream that runs from the Ain el Qilt gorge down to Jericho. It always has a flock of sheep and goats enjoying its shade.

Then, in verse 4, the opposite of blessing is described, in the opposite order: first comes the image, chaff blown away by the wind, then the description of the wicked. Finally, the last verse sums it all up with a neat contrast.

Psalm 2: Why do the nations conspire?

Originally this psalm was a coronation song. The death of a king and the succession of a new monarch was frequently the signal for rebellion by subject peoples, whom the Lord here 'laughs to scorn' (as Handel's *Messiah* puts it), for the Lord himself has decreed and anointed the new king. The ritual of kingship in Jerusalem took over much of the Egyptian coronation ritual. On the great Egyptian wall-carvings the king is shown being anointed and crowned by the deities of Upper and Lower Egypt. In the Egyptian ritual of coronation, the king was also adopted as son of the gods.

In Israel, of course, this divine sonship had a different root – God's promise to David, through Nathan, of a dynasty that would never end (2 Samuel 7:4–17). David offered to build a house for the Lord, but the Lord replied with a promise to build David a house, with his own son as his successor: 'I shall be a father to him,' he promised, 'and he a son to me' (v. 14). Though the Lord might punish the king, he would never withdraw his love. This promise is the basis of Israel's security and of the enduring hope for a Messiah who would rule the nations. The same promise is celebrated in another coronation psalm, Psalm 109[110[, and is frequently alluded to elsewhere in the Bible. During the exile, Psalm 88[89] meditates on the failure of the kingship and reproaches God for reneging on his promise.

The Christian tradition, beginning with the letter to the Hebrews (1:5), sees this promise as fulfilled in Christ. Perhaps even earlier, in the prayer of the apostles under persecution in Jerusalem (Acts 4:25–26), the Greek translation of 'his Anointed' ('his Christ') in Psalm 2:2 is used to identify the risen Christ as this anointed Messiah.

Jesus himself was hesitant about the title 'son of God', never openly accepting it. When Peter at last recognises Jesus as 'the Christ', Jesus reacts not with congratulations but with a warning that he is to triumph only after suffering (Mark 8:29–31). When the high priest challenges Jesus, 'Are you the Christ?' Jesus replies by diverting attention to his favourite title, 'the son of man' (Mark 14:61–62). This is probably because of the political associations of the concept of Messiah at the time, as an anointed king who would expel the Romans. For Jesus, it is not his own kingship but the kingship of God that fills his horizon.

Nevertheless, as early as Paul, 'Christ' (the Greek equivalent of the Hebrew 'Messiah') had become a standard name for Jesus. At Antioch, the great Jewish colony on the coast of Syria where Paul set up his first base for the proclamation of the gospel, the followers of Jesus first gained the name (possibly a slightly derisory nickname) 'Christians' – those who acclaimed Jesus as Messiah. They saw in Jesus the fulfilment of the anointed king promised in this psalm.

After the opening Wisdom psalm (Psalm 1), this psalm is really the beginning of the first book of Psalms. A royal, Davidic and messianic psalm is a feature of the seams between the five books of the Psalter.

Psalm 3: How many are my foes, O Lord!

In this psalm, the title is verse 1.

This is the first of the 'Psalms of David', a series that runs to Psalm 40[41]. The title added later at the head of each of these psalms attributes them to David and usually situates them at some particular moment in David's life. These indications are not to be taken too seriously. The situating of this psalm, 'When he was fleeing from his son Absalom' (that is, when Absalom had rebelled against his father and made a bloodless entry into Jerusalem, 2 Samuel 15:23–33), is particularly forced.

This is also the first of the psalms of confidence in distress, a frequent motif in prayer. It raises again the unanswerable question of how the psalms were preserved and used. Were psalm sheets kept in the temple and handed out on request to worshippers who asked for a particular type of prayer? That seems too modern an idea. In any case, we cannot tell. Sometimes the psalms seem to concentrate too much on the negative side of life. However, we are all drawn more quickly to prayer by threats to our comfort and prosperity! The calm confidence of the psalmist, who is content to brave the threats of the surrounding legions of enemies and go quietly to sleep, is a model for Christian trust in the Lord.

'I shall awake, for the Lord sustains me' (v. 5) is, by extension, understood in the Christian tradition as an allusion to Christ's resurrection. The verb used for 'awake' in the Greek is often used also of the resurrection. The doctrine of the resurrection of the dead becomes clear only in Daniel 12:2–3, written a couple of centuries before Christ, but the Greek Bible (particularly in the psalms) shows many signs of a tradition developing towards that belief. The translations chosen for the Greek Bible (the original Bible of the Christian Church) are a valuable indication of the developments of thinking within Judaism, and many regard the so-called Septuagint as an inspired translation. There is a longing for the continuance of a relationship with God instead of the unsatisfactory, powerless half-life in Sheol, where no one can praise God. With this longing goes a groping towards the belief in resurrection, in the form of a conviction that God will not abandon his chosen ones. Our link to God is a permanent, not a transitory, relationship. To God, all are still alive, even those from remote ages. As Jesus says in reply to the Sadducees, 'He is God, not of the dead, but of the living' (Matthew 22:32).

Psalm 4: When I call, answer me, O God of my righteousness

In this psalm, the title is verse 1.

This psalm is built on a contrast between trust in the Lord to provide what is needed and a certain materialistic preoccupation with acquiring the good things of this world. The psalmist is confident that the Lord hears prayers and grants what is needed. The opening mention of 'distress' is hardly sufficient to suggest upset or discomfort; it simply makes us aware that the Lord's protection is needed and is forthcoming.

The psalmist is sure that the Lord works wonders for his faithful ones; the Lord 'listens when I call to him' (v. 4). What exactly is this sureness of answer to prayer, and can we count on it so securely? How does God manage it if I want a fine day for my cricket match and the neighbouring farmer wants rain for his crops? A mature Christian may still desperately want something and pray for it fervently, but all the while his or her prayer includes an implied conditional clause: 'if it is your will and plan'. The mature Christian is still a child of God, turning to the Father in confidence but also in realisation that no human being can fully understand God's purposes. The sufferers who go in fervent and desperate prayer to a healing shrine such as Lourdes may not be granted the cure they seek but do win at least the strength to endure, and perhaps to understand, the suffering. In the last analysis there will always be cases where the book of Job provides the only solution: we cannot understand God's reasons but are made strong and trustful enough to bow before the vision of his wisdom and greatness.

By contrast, those who do not have this confidence are heavy of heart and chase after illusions, all the while complaining that no one offers them happiness. There is a touch of humour in the contrast between their frenetic and grumbling pursuit of happiness and the psalmist's contented and simple relaxation in the Lord. There is also a touch of irony in the fact that these seekers after happiness in material wealth also invoke the Lord in their search, expecting to be given such happiness on a plate, and asking to bask in the light of his face. Yet their plentiful harvest of corn and new wine does not bring them the contentment that the psalmist wins by trust in God.

The mention of keeping silence 'on your beds' (v. 5), and of falling asleep and resting secure (v. 9), suggests that the time of praying is evening, after a day spent in awareness of divine protection. In St Benedict's arrangement of the Psalms, this belongs to the monastic night prayer of Compline.

Psalm 5: To my words give ear, O Lord

In this psalm, the title is verse 1.

This is a simple morning prayer, rejoicing in the protection of the Lord at daybreak, contrasting the favour of the Lord toward his faithful with the Lord's detestation of evildoers, liars and the violent. The psalmist has a reassuring confidence in God's response to prayer and the closeness of God to those who come to pray to him. There is, however, a note that falls badly on the Christian ear – the appeal to God for judgment on the evildoers' guilt. It is not even an appeal for personal vengeance on unfair treatment, but seems quite unprovoked – apart from a passing reference to 'those who lie in wait for me' (v. 9).

It is possible to consider this jarring note as an expression of the desire for the annihilation of evil itself, a pious prayer that justice may triumph. More honest, however, is the admission that this desire for vengeance does exist in Old Testament morality. 'An eye for an eye, and a tooth for a tooth' (Deuteronomy 19:21b) was already an advance on a morality where there were no limits to revenge exacted, where someone could be killed for the sake of an eye or a tooth.

The Psalter leaves no doubt that Israel found it reasonable actually to pray for vengeance, as the so-called 'cursing psalms' show. The haunting Psalm 136[137] ends with a blessing on those who dash Babylonian babies against a rock, and Psalm 108[109] is (from the literary point of view) a deliciously and artistically comprehensive curse on the psalmist's enemies.

It was Jesus who outlawed all forms of revenge, with his command to 'love your enemies and pray for those who persecute you' (Matthew 5:44). The desire for vengeance is a very deep-seated human instinct. We must, furthermore, grant that revelation is a slow process and, at the same time, admit that we have no reason to believe that we have yet have reached the full implications of Christ's teaching. We cannot take on board too much at one time. Despite the implications of Pauline teaching, for many centuries Christendom continued to tolerate slavery and enjoy its benefits. For many centuries war and its accompanying slaughter were considered an acceptable last resort for solving disagreements under certain circumstances (the criteria of 'just war' theory). The suitability of the death penalty as the ultimate punishment is also still debated among Christians and non-Christians alike.

Psalm 6: O Lord, do not reprove me in your anger

In this psalm, the title is verse 1.

This is the first of the psalms of real distress, expressed with extreme drama or perhaps even exaggeration. Then suddenly it issues in a sharp turnaround, to confidence that the Lord has heard the prayer and already solved the problem.

These two phases are characterised respectively by the Lord's anger and his faithful love. The psalmist does not deny that punishment is due, but begs to be spared and appeals to God's faithful love, finally thanking God for deliverance from the threatening disasters. How can these two fit together?

The anger of the Lord is, of course, an anthropomorphism. Another anthropomorphic expression for it is the Lord's 'jealousy'. Frequent enough is the declaration that God is a jealous God. Divine jealousy is not like human jealousy. Human jealousy is hankering after qualities or possessions that one sees in others. Divine jealousy is a refusal to tolerate the attribution to others of the honour or obedience due to God, particularly if such honour is attributed to other deities – personifications of other systems of value. It is a refusal, therefore, to tolerate upset in the due order of the world, of which God is the ultimate guarantor. God's 'anger' is the attribution to God of the human emotion that so often precedes and occasions punishment. However, human anger so often involves the notion of losing one's temper that some translations use the expression 'wrath' of God, making it a quasi-technical term to avoid the implication that God has somehow 'lost the plot'.

The paradox is at its sharpest in the revelation to Moses at Sinai of the meaning of God's special, personal name. After the Israelites have broken the covenant and Moses has smashed the tablets of the Law, God passes before Moses crying out, 'The Lord, the Lord, God of tenderness and compassion, slow to anger, rich in faithful love and constancy... yet letting nothing go unchecked, and punishing...' (Exodus 34:6-7). This is the definition of God that echoes through scripture, alluded to again and again throughout the Old Testament. The paradox consists in the juxtaposition of compassion and punishment. How can God punish and yet be compassionate? Is God's forgiving punishment less severe than it should be? Hardly, if the punishment is intended to be therapeutic. Perhaps it is like a loving parent who punishes to bring the recalcitrant child back to the true path, but can lighten the punishment without reducing its effect by simultaneously showing the reality of his or her love, in some way sharing the child's pain.

Psalm 7: O Lord, my God, I take refuge in you

In this psalm, the title is verse 1.

This psalm may be seen as falling into three distinct but related parts. Verses 2–6 form an appeal to the Lord for protection, suggesting that the psalmist is being pursued by someone whom he attacked, though the attack does not seem to have been unprovoked. Verses 7–13a appeal to God specifically as a just judge, who can be relied on to reward integrity and punish the opposite. Verses 13b–17 somewhat return to the first part, stressing the justice of God in foiling the unprovoked attack of an enemy. Finally the psalmist sums up the prayer in a verse of praise for God's saving justice.

God's justice is understood throughout the Bible in two senses. Firstly, God is a just judge in the ordinary sense of the word, assessing merits and faults and assigning their just rewards; this is the sense found in the second part of the psalm. Secondly, but perhaps more importantly, God's justice is a saving justice. It is often put in parallel with 'salvation' or 'deliverance', as in Isaiah 46:13, 'I am bringing my *justice* nearer… my *salvation* will not delay.' The two nouns are obviously in parallel.

Human justice consists in conformity with the law (observing speed limits) or moral demands (repaying debts), but God's justice is conformity to his own promises. For the Israelite, and subsequently for the Christian, God's saving justice does not condemn us for our failures but quite the reverse: it is our only hope. God can be relied upon to fulfil his promises, especially the promises made to Abraham and the promises involved in the series of subsequent covenants to David and Jeremiah, and finally the new covenant in Christ's blood. All we can do is put our trust in this saving justice of God.

Paul meditates on this saving justice in the letter to the Romans: 'Abraham put his faith in God and this was reckoned to him as saving justice' (4:3). Human 'justice' cannot be earned by good deeds but is simply a matter of hanging on by our fingertips to God's saving justice – that is, trusting in his promises to save. We are justified – that is, put in a state of salvation – only by being clothed with God's own saving justice. In the last analysis, God's promises are fulfilled by Jesus' obedience on the cross, which 'fulfils all justice'. We profess our faith in and our dependence on that obedience by being baptised into Christ's death, and so bathed with his saving justice.

Psalm 8: O Lord, our Lord, how majestic is your name!

In this psalm, the title is verse 1.

This joyful psalm is a celebration of creation, bracketed at beginning and end by praise of God's majestic power. The first creation story in Genesis has the appearance of narrating what happened long, long ago. In fact, it is a theological statement in story form of the present, permanent relationship of the universe as we know it to the divine power that even now holds it in being. Psalm 8 is not an account but a celebration of that relationship. By its very being, the creation praises God: even the mouths of infants who cannot yet articulate words praise God in a way quite sufficient to confound his enemies.

Three little points may add to our appreciation of this psalm. First, the order differs from the account in Genesis. Human beings remain the crown of creation, made in God's image, but the order is different. In Genesis, the climax comes at the end of the creation story; here, human beings come immediately after the creation of the heavens and are followed, not preceded, by the animal creation. This bears some similarity to Genesis 2:20, where Adam completes God's work of creation by naming the animals and so giving them their intelligible nature.

Second, what are we to think of the phrase 'little less than the gods' (v. 6)? Is this an assertion that other gods exist? No; rather, it is using the language of the surrounding peoples and indeed the Canaanites, who honoured or worshipped a variety of divinities. Baal, the chief god of Canaan, was a storm-god, represented as hurling a bolt of forked lightning. Often, Hebrew literary forms lean towards such language, sometimes comparing these gods to the Lord, sometimes downgrading them to the status of angels. The letters to the Colossians and Ephesians take stock of the situation explicitly: in Christ everything has its being. 'Everything visible and everything invisible, thrones, ruling forces, sovereignties, powers – all things were created through him and in him' (Colossians 1:16).

Third, the psalm is playfully anthropomorphic: the heavens were shaped by the fingers of God (v. 4). The beginning and end are more theological: the praise is given to the name of the Lord. The name of the Lord bespeaks the divine power. When God reveals the meaning of his name to Moses (Exodus 34:5-7), he reveals the nature of his saving power. In Isaiah we read, 'I am the Lord; that is my name! I shall not yield my glory to another' (42:8). In the same way, in Acts, Christians are baptised 'into the name of the Lord Jesus' (see 10:48; 19:5), and are those over whom the name of Jesus has been called. That is, Christians are those who put themselves under the power of Jesus.

Psalm 9[9—10]: I will praise you, Lord, with all my heart

In this psalm, the title is verse 1.

Here begins the dislocation of numbering, for Psalm 9 in the Greek version is divided into Psalms 9 and 10 by the Hebrew. The Greek version, the original Bible of the Christian Church, represents the state of the Hebrew in the second century before Christ, so the division in the present Hebrew text must have been made after that.

Further indication that the whole poem was originally one comes from the lettering. The psalm is an alphabetical psalm – that is, each quatrain begins with a different letter of the Hebrew alphabet, working through from beginning to end. In other psalms the same neat device is used – for example, in Psalms 111[112] and 112[113] there is a new letter for each line; in Psalm 118[119] stanzas of eight lines begin with the same letter.

The psalm is redolent with the spirituality of the Lord's care for the orphan, the oppressed, the needy and the poor. Although God's care for the poor is a theme that runs throughout Israel's literature, pre-exilic spirituality is rather more robust: material success is a blessing from the Lord. From the exile onwards, Israel was more conscious of its own failures and of its continuously oppressed state. The exiles had lost their confidence and concentrated on their guilt, continually expressing their repentance. This was reinforced by circumstances. First there was the state of servitude in the Babylonian exile. Then, after the return to Judea, came harassment from those who had stayed behind or had been transported there, and oppression by one foreign power after another – Greeks, Egyptians, Syrians, Romans. So in their enforced humility the Israelites saw that this itself was a blessing, that the blessing of the Lord is upon those who trust not in themselves but in God's own saving power. The poor of the Lord are under the shelter of his wings and under the special blessing of his hand.

This spirituality receives its full expression in the prophets of this period, especially Zephaniah. The poor of the Lord are those who accept this state of dependence and put all their trust in God's power and willingness to save: 'Seek the Lord, all you humble of the earth' (Zephaniah 2:3). God declares, 'I shall leave surviving a humble and lowly people, and those who are left in Israel will take refuge in the name of the Lord' (3:12–13). This line of thought runs straight through to the Beatitudes in Luke ('Blessed are you who are poor', 6:20) and to Mary's canticle of the Magnificat.

Psalm 10[11]: In the Lord I have taken refuge

This psalm of confidence is based on the presence of the Lord among his people. Is this presence 'in heaven' or 'in his holy temple' (v. 4)? The lines and the thoughts are in parallel, a frequent phenomenon in Hebrew poetry – or, rather, the one widespread structural element of Hebrew poetry. While English poetry often achieves its balance by a rhyming syllable at the end of the line, Hebrew poetry gains its balance by parallelism. Two lines make roughly the same statement: for example, 'O God, come to my assistance // O Lord, make haste to help me.' Sometimes one of the two statements is phrased negatively: 'Lord, deliver me from my enemies // do not let them triumph over me.' This gives a satisfying rhythm. In the case of this psalm, whether the Lord is in his temple or in the heavens, the assertion is that the Lord is in control.

The psalm expresses in several different ways the protective presence of God. This is a fundamental theme in the Bible. His eyes watch over the world (v. 4) and, conversely, the upright will ever see his face (v. 7). On Sinai Israel experienced the presence of God among them, choosing them to be his own people. He remained present among them, and Moses went to consult him at the ark of the covenant, housed in the middle of the camp, in the tent of meeting. It was an awesome encounter. The splendour of the Lord was such that Moses subsequently had to keep his face veiled (Exodus 34:33): 'the Israelites could not look Moses steadily in the face' (2 Corinthians 3:7). When David had captured Jerusalem and made it his capital, he made it also God's capital by bringing the ark, the presence of God, into Jerusalem. It was a protecting presence but a presence not to be trifled with, as the fate of Uzzah showed (2 Samuel 6:7).

In the gospels it is perhaps Matthew who most stresses this presence, which is now the divine presence of Jesus in his Church. Jesus' name, 'Emmanuel', means 'God with us' (Matthew 1:23); in 18:20, Jesus promises to the Church, 'Where two or three meet in my name, I am there among them.' Again in Matthew, corresponding to the initial bracket of 'Emmanuel' is the final bracket, as Jesus, the risen Lord and glorious Son of Man, sends out his apostles, promising, 'I am with you always, to the end of time' (28:20).

Psalm 11[12]: Save me, O Lord

In this psalm, the title is verse 1.

The sadness that the psalmist feels here stems from being enmeshed in a web of lies. To be misrepresented or misunderstood is an ultimate frustration, and here it seems that the false representation is being passed round deliberately, maliciously and rapidly. A right to truth and a good reputation is one of the basic human rights, without which no security is possible. It is one of the major social values, put forward by the Ten Commandments themselves, and the psalmist longs for it, contrasting the web of lies with the purity of God's truth, truthfulness and trustworthiness – to which he applies the lovely image of sparkling silver 'seven times refined' (v. 7).

Another 'gold standard' (or perhaps we should say 'silver standard') enters into the calculations here, namely salvation. The first word of the psalm is 'Save!' and verse 6 repeats this confidence in the Lord's 'salvation'. Here the salvation envisaged is obviously rescue from deceit and misrepresentation, but in Christian prayer the concept is used widely and often thoughtlessly. What does God save us from? From hell, from evil, from slavery to sin, from enemies, from poverty and oppression, from ourselves? Is the basic worry about threatening disaster an unnecessary pessimism for Christians? The image of God as Saviour stems originally from God's rescue of Moses and his people from slavery in Egypt – the great salvation of the exodus. A repetition of this rescue was Israel's expectation in the dark days of the Babylonian exile.

Primarily the Saviour is God, for the title is transferred to Jesus only rarely in the New Testament. In the gospels it is used almost exclusively by Luke. He uses the concept of Jesus (the name means 'Saviour') in contrast to the saviour-gods of the Roman world. In that uncertain world of unpredictable disaster, it was common to be initiated into cults of mysterious magical deities that promised stability and safety. Luke presents Jesus as the only true Saviour. Jesus travels through Galilee rescuing people from all the fears of sickness, death, alienation, addiction, unknown and threatening powers and taboos, emptying the worm-can of fear. Whatever we fear, Jesus is ultimately the guarantor of liberty and safety.

Psalm 12[13]: O Lord, will you forget me forever?

In this psalm, the title is verse 1.

In this neat little psalm the psalmist is intensely personally preoccupied. In almost every line, 'I', 'me' or 'my' occurs. It is an energetic, vigorous poem, and its thought advances by hammering repetition. First comes a fourfold 'How long…?' (vv. 2–3). Then there are three insistent imperatives – 'look', 'answer', 'give light' (v. 4) – followed by three dangers to be avoided: 'Lest… lest… lest' ('or I shall fall… or my foe will boast… my enemy have the joy of seeing me stumble, vv. 4b–6). Only after this fusillade of hammer-blows does the psalmist relax in the final verse by putting all trust in the salvation and in the *hesed* of God.

This *hesed* is a key concept for Israel. It is normally translated 'faithful love' or 'merciful love', but it is a concept that grips and warms the heart. In origin it is the love that binds together a close and devoted family, in which every member can count on the inalienable support of each one. The concept is enshrined in Israel's family law, protecting against ultimate disaster. If a brother marries and dies without children, his brother must marry the widow and raise up a child in the dead brother's name. If a brother falls on such hard times that he is forced to sell his share of the ancestral land, the nearest brother must buy it back for him. Each member of the family can rely on the fact that they may not get on very well with one another but, in the last analysis, they won't let each other down. *Hesed* is the love of the mother who will never turn her child away, whatever hurt the child does to her. So unalterable is God's love, the love of the father for the prodigal son, and that is why we can 'trust in your faithful love'.

Hosea is the prophet of such love, and it is from Hosea 6:6 that Jesus takes his text, 'What I want is love, not sacrifice.' In Matthew this principle is stated twice (9:13; 12:7), forming the touchstone for the application of the Law. The Father's unalterable love does not spawn a formal, ritual response, but evokes a heartfelt, reciprocal love of God and of the neighbour as oneself.

Psalm 13[14]: The fool has said in his heart

This is a Wisdom psalm, teaching about folly and wisdom. It is built on a contrast, with the turning point in the middle of verse 4; the first half describes the wicked, the second half those whom the Lord will save.

The fool in the first half, who says in his heart, 'There is no God', is not a deep-thinking atheist announcing a carefully considered opinion. There are many sorts of fool, and the word used here for 'fool' (*nabal*) is more of a coarse lout, who understands nothing and is rough and insensitive. The perfect example of this sort of person is Nabal, the rich and loutish landowner in 1 Samuel 25, who refuses to pay David for guarding his crops ('Nabal is his name and *nabal* his nature,' says his wife, as she prepares to snuggle into David's bed). So the first part of the psalm characterises the insensitive lout, whose loutishness expresses itself in a practical inability to appreciate divine values.

The psalm stresses how widespread such fools are, with the triple 'No one who does any good... not one... not one'.

For Christians, this denunciation has an especial force because it is quoted by Paul in Romans 3, when he is summing up the depravity of all humanity – first Gentiles, then Jews – with a string of scriptural quotations. After outlining the failure of Gentiles to obey natural law and the failure of Jews to obey the Law of Moses, Paul emphasises that this is not surprising, giving six scriptural quotations about the utter depravity of the human race. This is the depravity from which we are saved by Christ's obedient self-sacrifice: 'just as one man's trespass led to condemnation for all, so one man's act of righteousness leads to justification and life for all' (Romans 5:18, NRSV).

The second half of the psalm, however, is more hopeful. It gives the three groups of people whom the Lord will protect and rescue. First (v. 5), there is 'the righteous generation' or, in less formal language, those who live according to God's Law, appreciating and endeavouring to live within its promises. Righteousness, of course, consists not in earning salvation – no one can do that – but in reliance on God's promises. Second (v. 6), there are the poor – those who, having no resources of their own, turn to God for help. Third (v. 7), all Israel will draw salvation from Zion.

Psalm 14[15]: Lord, who may abide in your tent?

This psalm is a little litany of requirements for keeping company with God. Some commentators have interpreted it rather woodenly as a sort of interrogation to be conducted at the door of the sanctuary. It is more a reflection on the moral qualities required, somewhat similar to Psalm 1, a typical and comforting Wisdom psalm. To describe the list as a set of ten commandments goes, perhaps, a little too far. The qualities are expressed first positively, in terms of what we should do (vv. 2, 4), and then negatively – what we should not do (vv. 3, 5). The first set of qualities concerns telling the truth; the second centres on business dealings. Both sets are as relevant to today's world as to the world of the original psalmist. So often, public morality seems to approve anything you can get away with. If you can win your case by concealing or twisting evidence, that is considered fair play. If fraudulent financial dealings are well enough disguised, that is considered fair game. The morality outlined by the psalmist goes much further.

It is, however, the first line that I find arresting, with the words 'abide in your tent'. The psalmist is phrasing closeness to God in terms of the tent of meeting. During the desert wanderings, the tent of meeting was the mobile sanctuary where God would reveal himself, where the Lord would 'talk to Moses face to face, as a man talks to his friend' (Exodus 33:11). Israel always yearned for the simplicity of the desert relationship with the Lord, which they saw as the honeymoon period when Israel was faithful to the Lord. There is a richness about desert spirituality that cannot be rivalled. When you are alone in the desert, you have no artificial support or distraction. It can be both daunting and inspiring. It certainly leads to focus and self-knowledge, and to that wonderful relationship, 'fear of the Lord'.

The verb used in the Hebrew for 'abide' or 'dwell' is the word from which the *shekinah* of the Lord is derived, a word full of dread and mystery – that awesome glory of the Lord that no human being can look upon. It is the word to which the prologue of John's gospel refers: 'the Word was made flesh and *dwelt* among us'. The word itself has overtones of peace, tranquillity and confidence in the Lord. The whole psalm is about dwelling with the Lord and cannot but call to mind the words of Jesus: 'Those who abide in me and I in them bear much fruit' (John 15:5, NRSV).

Psalm 15[16]: O Lord, it is you who are my portion and cup

To avoid the accusation of neglecting problems, a preliminary word must be said about verses 3–4: they are very obscure, and the text differs in Greek and Hebrew. The mention of 'holy ones in the land' and 'other gods' may imply that the author once revered some earth deities or agricultural spirits, from whom he has now turned to worship the Lord with all his heart.

The main theme, however, is delight in the Lord, perhaps by contrast to the earth deities. The phrase 'you who are my portion and cup' (v. 5) expresses the firm and lasting link between God and the psalmist. In the Christian further understanding of the psalm, it is even often understood as an allusion to the sacramental, eucharistic cup that mediates the presence of Christ – a legitimate application, though it was certainly not part of the original sense of the psalm.

In its own Old Testament context, therefore, this is one of the passages in the Psalms that express the longing for eternal company with the Lord, and a belief that God will not abandon forever those who commit themselves to him. The psalmist cannot rest satisfied with the powerless half-life of Sheol, where it is impossible even to praise God. Exactly what the psalmist hopes for is not yet clear. Does 'my body shall rest in safety' (v. 9) imply a hope of bodily resurrection? This hope becomes explicit only in the book of Daniel, less than two centuries before Christ. As with similar mentions in the book of Psalms, it is unclear whether the psalmist is hoping to be rescued from Sheol in the sense of being brought back from Sheol, or in the sense of having the descent to Sheol indefinitely postponed. In either case, his hope is founded on the strong and permanent bond of affection that God has for his chosen ones. God so loves and protects them that he can never abandon any of them to see corruption.

Furthermore, in Peter's speech at Pentecost (Acts 2:25–31; see also 13:35), a full quotation of verses 8–11 is used to prove the resurrection of Christ: 'You will not... allow your holy one to see corruption.' In the New Testament, the resurrection of Christ is always seen as the template and model of the resurrection of the Christian, who is baptised into Christ's death and raised in Christ's resurrection. These verses therefore must be seen as a full and confident acclamation of our destiny to Christian resurrection.

Psalm 16[17]: O Lord, hear a cause that is just

This confident prayer follows the previous psalm in much the same spirit, secure in the conviction that God will save, and also ending with a firm expectation of final permanent company with the Lord: 'behold your face... with the vision of your presence' (v. 15). To see the face of the Lord is a bold way of expressing tranquil enjoyment of the divine presence. In the vision of the new Jerusalem with which the book of Revelation concludes, 'the throne of God and of the Lamb will be in the city; his servants will worship him; they will see him face to face' (Revelation 22:3–4).

One difference from the previous psalm is that, here, the psalmist is threatened by enemies. Indeed, it may be helpful to imagine him in the same situation as the prophet Jeremiah. Jeremiah was constrained to make himself unpopular as the Babylonian forces advanced to sack Jerusalem in 587BC. He graphically foretold the disaster that would follow if the nation continued in its stubborn refusal to return to the Lord, and was duly persecuted and imprisoned for his pains, being dumped in the mud of an almost empty storage-well. The king had a good deal of sympathy for him, but was obviously constricted by his army officers and could help Jeremiah only secretly. The book of Jeremiah contains a series of poems in which Jeremiah complains to the Lord about the uncongenial task he has been given, protesting his loyalty but bemoaning the persecution it brings with it (for example, Jeremiah 20:7–18). This psalm similarly circles round the theme of confidence in divine protection against enemies who are pressing upon the psalmist.

The sequence of the psalm may be seen as fivefold, parts one, three and five being declarations of confidence in the Lord, each special in its way. So we see the structure:

- Verses 1–2: Confidence in the Lord, based on 'my justice'. As we have noted, this is not a complacent protestation of perfect behaviour, but a trust in God's fidelity to his promises: Abraham trusted in God and this was accounted to him as justice.
- Verses 3–5: A declaration of fidelity – by contrast to the violence of the enemy.
- Verses 6–8: Confidence in the Lord. This is enthusiastic, almost wild. Verse 7a could be translated as an explosive 'Make a wonderful demonstration of your faithful love (*hesed*)'.
- Verses 9–13: The enemy on the prowl, centred on the image of lions prowling round the camp at night, a blood-freezing experience.
- Verses 14–15: Confidence in the Lord – the final face-to-face vision of God and a triumphant ending to the prayer.

Psalm 17[18]: I love you, Lord my strength

In this psalm, the title is verse 1.

This is one of the longest of the psalms; in fact, only two are longer. Another feature is that it comes almost identically in an appendix to the story of David, in 2 Samuel 22. All the psalms were traditionally, of course, attributed to David, and most of them certainly falsely. Whether this one had David as its author or not, most of it nicely fits the life of David. Other divisions are possible, but to me it is most attractive to divide the psalm into two distinct halves, joined by the bridge of verses 21–25. This bridge itself is strongly reminiscent of the book of Deuteronomy, for it concentrates on observance of the Law ('the ways of the Lord', his 'judgments', 'blameless', 'kept from guilt', hands 'clean in his eyes'). The poems before and after are of a different stamp. The two halves are also connected at beginning and end by the strong stress on God as Rock (vv. 3 and 47), a dominant emphasis in each poem.

The first 20 verses form an energetic account of God's divine intervention, using the traditional Canaanite language and imagery of God as a deity of storm and nature. Baal, the chief god of Canaan before Israel's arrival, is always represented as a storm-god, hurling a thunderbolt. This is the imagery also of the divine encounter on Sinai, when the appearance of God to Moses and the Israelites is described in terms of thunder, lightning and earthquake (Exodus 19:16–18). At least in a world without explosives or nuclear fission, these were the most awesome manifestations of power imaginable. The uncontrollable force of hurricanes, tornados and tsunamis is unstoppable even by modern precautions. They remain the most powerful image of the divine might. In the first 20 verses, this is the irresistible might that seizes David and saves him. Perhaps it might be considered a poetic commentary on the divine intervention in David's contest with Goliath.

The final section (vv. 26–51) is a vigorous celebration of how God – again as Rock – equipped and trained the psalmist as a victorious warrior. Today we would not perhaps celebrate with such gusto how the warrior crushed his enemies 'fine, like dust before the wind' (NRSV). More suitable would be to adopt the Pauline application of the language of the Roman gladiatorial contests – the contemporary equivalent of football matches – to the armour of God in Ephesians 6:13–17, with the shield of faith as a sure defence against the burning arrows of the Evil One, and the word of God as a two-edged sword.

Psalm 18[19]: The heavens declare the glory of God

In this psalm, the title is verse 1.

At first sight, this psalm consists of two independent psalms, one about the heavens, the other about the Law of the Lord. As is obvious, they are in different rhythms and lengths of line. However, it is also attractive to see the psalm as one continuous threefold whole: God speaks through the glory of the heavens; the Lord speaks through his revelation of the Law; the believer speaks in response.

The opening section of the psalm celebrates, first, the heavens declaring the glory of God by their unlimited expanse. Especially with our modern knowledge of the vast distances of space and the ever-expanding universe, it is impossible to look up at the night skies without being overawed by the Creator or without appreciating the littleness of the human race. Then the psalm celebrates the sun, rising and traversing the heavens. Today we might not celebrate the sun in just these terms, yet we cannot but be aware of the beneficent influence exerted by it and of our dependence on it. Contrast a cold and perishing world without the sun! In the first line of the psalm, the word for 'God' is 'El', the common word for a god; here we are celebrating the natural creation. In the second section of the psalm, the name will be YHWH, Israel's own special name for Israel's God. In verses 8–15 it is repeated seven times, the perfect number.

The second section of the psalm celebrates the special revelation of God to Israel, given in the Law, by which YHWH gives Israel both life and wisdom. The Law given to Israel on Sinai is not constricting but is liberating, for it shows how Israel may live as God's people, in the image of God and representing God to the world. They are shown the way to 'be holy as I am holy' (Leviticus 19:2). They are shown how to respect, revere and love the glory of God ('the fear of the Lord is pure', v. 10). They are shown how to respect and give dignity and life to other human beings ('You will treat resident aliens as though they were native-born and love them as yourself – for you yourselves were once aliens in Egypt', Leviticus 19:34). This is why the precepts of the Lord are more to be desired than gold, and sweeter than honey.

In the final verse, after the heavens have spoken of the glory of God, after God has revealed himself by speaking his Law, the psalmist asks that his own words may win favour with God, his Rock.

A feature of this group of psalms has been that most of them are private prayers, rather than prayers for public assemblies or prayers reflecting on God's care of Israel throughout history. Repeatedly God is hailed as 'my Rock', 'my Refuge'. Basically, prayer is a personal and private matter, an intimate love affair, in which we open ourselves to God's love and God nourishes our relationship to him, drawing us close to himself and revealing himself to us in the silence of our inmost being.

Psalm 19[20]: May the Lord answer in time of trial

In this psalm, the title is verse 1.

This psalm is often considered a coronation psalm. The first six verses are good wishes or congratulations to the king, rather than prayers. The last four verses express confidence in the Lord's patronage of the king, his anointed.

Scholars have attempted to pinpoint a particular king, the most likely focus being upon Josiah, although Josiah is only one possibility. He was king of Judah from 640 to 609BC, at the time of the Babylonian threat which was to destroy Jerusalem a decade after his death. This would account for the suggestion of danger in verse 1, 'in time of trial', and the assertions of confidence of victory in war. More persuasive is the insistence on the power of the name of the Lord (vv. 2, 6, 8). At this time, the time of the Deuteronomic reform under Josiah, there was considerable stress on the name of the Lord, standing for the power of the Lord. The name of the Lord is itself glorious and awe-inspiring (Deuteronomy 28:58). The Lord has placed his name to dwell in the temple of Jerusalem, meaning that his power is accessible there. However, a stress on the power of the name of the Lord is not confined to this period.

The psalm brings to mind the stress on the power of the name of the Lord Jesus in the New Testament and Christian context. Throughout Acts, Christians are baptised into the name of Jesus – that is, into the company of Jesus. All who call on the name of the Lord will be saved, says Peter at Pentecost (Acts 2:21). The followers of Jesus are known as those over whom the name of the Lord has been invoked or pronounced – fittingly, indeed, as they are known as 'Christians'. It is in the name of Jesus that Peter acts and works miracles (Acts 3:6). The name of Jesus designates the power in which Christians act more than 30 times in Acts. This has become the equivalent of the name of the Lord in the Old Testament.

The other key word that occurs three times in the second half of the psalm is 'salvation' (v. 7: 'the Lord saves his anointed… with the mighty salvation of his right hand'; v. 10: 'Grant salvation to the king, O Lord'). In the original, this was no doubt understood in terms of military deliverance. In Christian prayer, however, it will bear a wider sense, meaning the salvation for which we long and for which we rely on the Lord. Salvation from sickness? From the evil tendencies of which I am ashamed? From anything I fear? From myself? Any earthly salvation is a pale shadow of this ultimate gift.

Psalm 20[21]: In your strength, O Lord, the king rejoices

In this psalm, the title is verse 1.

Like the previous psalm, this is a prayer for the king, though it has less emphasis on the actual coronation, for it assumes that the king has already received the Lord's blessings. The structure may be regarded as twofold, verses 2, 8 and 14 being perhaps choral responses, while the intervening two sets of verses reflect on the blessings that the Lord has granted. The first set (vv. 3–7) reflects on his personal blessings, the second (vv. 9–13) on his military victories.

How should Christians pray this psalm in an age when the idea of war conjures up not merely individual heroism but death by 'friendly fire', mass destruction of civilians and other brutalising factors? Many, probably most, Christians would accept war as a very last resort, on the condition that the injustices and infringements of human rights it entails are less than in the alternative. In the Bible, wars, and even the slaughtering of enemies, are taken for granted. The most blood-chilling example is the slaughter of the prisoner-of-war Agag by Samuel in cold blood 'before the Lord' in 1 Samuel 15:33. War is, perhaps, the most extreme case of the gradual revelation and refinement of moral sensibilities. Just as truths about the relationship of God to human beings, in such matters as life after death, become clear only gradually, so do the moral teachings about how human beings should behave to one another. The Old Testament limited revenge: 'an eye [only] for an eye, and a tooth [only] for a tooth' (Exodus 21:24). In the Sermon on the Mount, Jesus bans revenge altogether (Matthew 5:39). The Old Testament permitted divorce and remarriage for 'fornication' (Deuteronomy 24:1), but Jesus bans it altogether (Mark 10:5–9).

Even the moral teaching of the New Testament on the love, respect and freedom due to each individual was, for many centuries, not seen by Christians as incompatible with slavery or forcible conversion. In praying this psalm and others that glory in slaughter, we can only ask that the world of today may be spared the hideous injustices of war, and be thankful for the gentle pressure of the Holy Spirit that has led us to a deeper understanding of the implications of biblical teaching. It is, after all, already there in the creation story, where human beings were created in the image of God to further and complete God's creation, not to destroy it. They were lapped in the peace of the garden of Eden. Even there, the guidance of the Spirit was required, for there human beings were free to eat the fruit of the plants. Meat-eating comes in only after the flood (Genesis 9:3), though this is not generally understood to prohibit the eating of meat.

Psalm 21[22]: My God, my God, why have you forsaken me?

In this psalm, the title is verse 1.

This psalm has a very special place in Christian prayer and devotion, for it is the psalm whose first words come on the lips of Jesus in his last agony on the cross in the gospels of Mark and Matthew. The evangelists draw attention also to the fulfilment of other passages in this psalm during the course of the passion narrative, such as verses 8–9 and 18–19. It has often been interpreted as a cry of despair, as though, under the weight of the sins of the world, Jesus felt himself utterly abandoned and cut off from his Father, God-forsaken in the fullest sense. This will not do, though, for the crucifixion is the moment when Jesus is most fully united to his Father in perfect love. It is the loving obedience of Jesus in accepting the Father's will that undoes the disobedience of Adam. As Paul shows in Romans 5, the obedience of the second Adam annuls and reconciles the disobedience of the first Adam (for 'Adam' means 'man' or 'humanity' as a whole). It is this filial obedience that leads the centurion to say, 'Truly, this man was Son of God' (Mark 15:39).

Understood in its context, this cry of Jesus should be seen not in isolation but as the intonation of the whole psalm, the beginning of the psalm which gives the whole sense of the passion of Jesus. This is reinforced from time to time by the other quotations from the psalm in the passion narrative. The psalm moves through the desolation and humiliation of the sufferer to the glory to God and the triumphant recognition of the sufferer. It is only through suffering and desolation that the servant of the Lord achieves not only the glory of God but also his personal vindication and triumph. Jesus' intonation of the first verse of the psalm shows that this is the spirit in which he underwent the cross, confident in the glory of God and his own vindication. God the Father 'will rescue my soul from the sword' (v. 21) and 'they shall praise the Lord, those who seek him' (v. 27). Such confidence did not, of course, lessen the suffering of this barbaric method of execution, but it gave the suffering a purpose.

This psalm is often called 'the Psalm of the Suffering Servant' from its similarity to the Song of the Suffering Servant in Isaiah 53. By his allusion to this song at the last supper (his blood 'poured out for many'), it is clear that Jesus saw himself as this Servant of the Lord, who came 'not to be served but to serve, and to give his life a ransom for many' (Matthew 20:28).

Psalm 22[23]: The Lord is my shepherd

There is an interesting and artistic balance in this psalm, of the pattern a-b-b-a. The first three verses reflect on the Lord as shepherd; then verse 4 addresses the Lord as shepherd directly, in the second person ('you'). In the latter half, the order is reversed: first the Lord is addressed directly ('you') as host, then the last verse is a further reflection on the Lord's welcome into his house.

The image of the shepherd gives the tone to this psalm, though by the third stanza the image has changed to the Lord as host, entertaining and comforting his guest. We like to think of sheep as frisky, cuddly lambs, but – like most of us – as they get older they get more difficult! Sheep are notoriously unpredictable, apt to dash helplessly across the road in front of any car, vulnerable, confused and in need of the most elementary guidance. In the steep valleys and rocky canyons of the Judean countryside, all too often one comes across the carcase of a sheep that went astray and ended up in the valley of the shadow of death.

In the countryside imagery of the gospels, sheep are a favourite, and this may serve as a commentary on the psalm. Perhaps the best-known passage is the parable of the lost sheep. This is applied by Matthew (18:12–15) to teach the duty of the Christian to search out and bring back any member of the community who has strayed, and by Luke (15:4–7) to teach the exhilarating joy of forgiveness. The image is used in the only parable in the gospel of John, that of the good shepherd (10:1–6). Here the generous love of Jesus' sacrifice, his devotion to the sheep who 'know his voice', is the point. It even distorts the image, for it is hardly an appropriate sacrifice of a shepherd to die for a sheep – presumably leaving the others untended.

A further use of the image is in the story of the feeding of the five thousand, and this even brings in the aspect of the Lord as host. Jesus begins by taking pity on the crowds 'because they were like sheep without a shepherd' (Mark 6:34). Then he feeds them on the green pastures beside the restful waters of the Sea of Galilee. This is the perfect picture of the shepherd giving food to his sheep, made more perfect by the eucharistic overtones of the piece. The Eucharist is always a gathering of Jesus and his disciples, and here we see the shepherd feeding his sheep as Jesus feeds his followers at the eucharistic table.

Psalm 23[24]: The Lord's is the earth and its fullness

A possible opinion is that this psalm was written for a liturgical procession of the ark of the covenant into the temple, perhaps annually. The first half would then be a sort of examination of conscience, not unlike Psalm 14[15], about who is worthy to participate in the procession, and the second half would be a liturgical lyric for the procession. The principal difficulty with this interpretation is that there is no suggestion anywhere that such a procession took place. Nor is the ark mentioned in this psalm. We know only that David brought the ark up to Jerusalem in the generation before the temple was built.

Whether this annual procession took place or not, the elevated and mythical language of the psalm is a reminder that, in the prayer of the liturgy, earth is joined to heaven. The action is hovering between two spheres. This is an aspect made particularly clear in the liturgy of the eastern churches. In these churches the numerous icons of the saints, and ceilings painted blue with golden stars, are intended as a reminder that heaven and its inhabitants surround us in our prayer and take part in it. The same is said to be the purpose of the soaring Gothic arches of medieval western cathedrals – to draw the mind up to heaven. In this psalm, the 'ancient doors' of the temple receive a poetic and mythical extension to make them yet higher as doors to the heavenly sanctuary, where the Lord of Hosts awaits us.

The meaning of the title 'YHWH Sebaoth' is not entirely clear. It occurs some dozen times in the Psalms, but most frequently in Isaiah (for example, 6:3, 5), where it is a title of the mighty God enthroned in the temple of Jerusalem. 'Sebaoth' has primarily military connotations, suggesting hosts of warriors, but in connection with YHWH it is often used of God surrounded by his councillors, the holy ones (Psalm 88[89]:6–9). God is imagined here as a mighty monarch, surrounded by serried ranks of courtiers who do his will. This is the picture familiar from ancient Mesopotamian mythology and the first chapter of the book of Job. It is a way of expressing the unlimited powers of God who directs the course of history by means of these unseen and incorporeal forces. Among them, of course, are the angels (the word means 'messengers'), who carry his self-accomplishing word to human beings.

Psalm 24[25]: To you, O Lord, I lift up my soul

This is the first of the acrostic psalms. English poetry often receives its form and balance from a rhyme at the end of the line. Hebrew poetry, on the other hand, often receives it from the letters of the alphabet at the start of the line. In this psalm, the verses begin successively with each of the letters of the Hebrew alphabet. The same structure occurs in other psalms, such as 110[111] and 111[112]. Psalm 118[119] is a special *tour de force*: each verse of the eight-verse sections begins with a successive letter of the alphabet. The acrostic pattern seems to be a feature of post-exilic poetry. Such a date for this psalm would also fit the spirituality of the period, with its consciousness of guilt and failure and its eagerness for instruction in complete observance of God's pleasure.

The shape of the psalm is concentric. At the outside is an envelope (vv. 2–3 and 20–21): the psalmist's trust and hope is in the Lord, so he should not be put to shame. In the central part of the psalm, two themes interweave:

- The theme of instruction in the ways of the Lord, so that the psalmist may fulfil the covenant (vv. 4–5, 8–9, 12–14). Here, words like 'teach', 'guide', 'paths' and 'ways' predominate.
- The theme of forgiveness (vv. 6–7, 15–19). Here, the dominant words are 'mercy' (*hesed*) and 'compassion'.

At the very centre come verses 10–11, where the two themes are combined – instruction in the way, and forgiveness for failure. Both of these, the plea for guidance and the need for forgiveness, are valuable topics also for Christian prayer.

Psalm 25[26]: Give judgment for me, O Lord

Let us begin with two easy misconceptions. This psalm is often regarded as a sort of entry liturgy, pronounced by someone coming to pray in the temple (perhaps at one of the great feasts), declaring his innocence on the threshold and his intention of cleansing his hands in innocence at the washing-fountain which presumably stood at the entrance to the temple – as it does now at the entrance to the Muslim Dome of the Rock, which occupies the position of the temple in Jerusalem. This scenario is unlikely, for in the Bible there are no instructions for such a ceremony and no evidence that it ever occurred. Nevertheless, some of us may find it helpful to imagine such a situation.

The second misconception is that the psalm is a complacent protestation of innocence, such as the self-satisfied Pharisee would have made in Luke's parable of the Pharisee and the tax collector (Luke 18:9–14). No, the psalmist is not complacent; yes, he does protest his innocence. He is trying his best, but he knows that he needs help.

Firstly, he is very much aware that he is still on the road: 'I have walked in my integrity' (v. 1 and again in v. 11, a nice bracket), 'I walk according to your truth' (v. 3), and 'My foot stands on level ground' (v. 12). This is all reminiscent of Hebrews 4:1–11, which insists that the Christian is still on pilgrimage and has not yet entered the place of rest which was promised at the end of the exodus wanderings.

Secondly, there is an appeal for redemption (v. 11). This image is often and aptly used to describe Christ's work (also called salvation, reconciliation and other images). The basic idea behind it is release from slavery. It often stands for buying back hostages or captives. In the Bible it usually refers to the Lord releasing his people from slavery in Egypt, purchasing them as slaves are purchased and making them his own people, to serve him alone. So the psalmist is praying that he may be released and purchased in the same way.

Thirdly, there is an appeal to the covenant of mercy. Verse 3 speaks of 'mercy' and 'truth', that pair of words which sets every bell of love and fidelity ringing. God's 'mercy' is his love, *hesed* – a family love, a forgiving love, the very definition of God's nature. And God's 'truth' is his truthfulness, in the sense of his fidelity to the promises he has made, which will never fail. We rely on this truthfulness for all his promises. It is the bedrock of Paul's letter to the Romans. It is the idea fulfilled in Jesus, the true shepherd, the true vine, the way, the truth and the life. The psalmist is not complacent but reliant.

Psalm 26[27]: The Lord is my light and my salvation

It is possible to argue that this psalm is formed from two psalms joined together, verses 1–6 and 7–14. The earlier half is more optimistic and confident, the later more threatened. On the other hand, there is a continuity of thought. Either this shows that the psalm is a single composition or it gives the reason why two disparate psalms were joined together! The idea of seeking the Lord is prominent in both parts (vv. 4, 8). The longing is similarly expressed: 'all the days of my *life* to gaze on the *beauty of the Lord*' (v. 4) and to 'see *the Lord's goodness* in the land of the *living*' (v. 13). In both parts there is a threat from enemies or foes (vv. 2, 6, 11). Who these foes are, we cannot know, but the images of threats facing the psalmist are so varied in the psalms that there is no need to deduce that actual warfare with an army (v. 3) is envisaged.

The striking feature of the psalm is the ardent desire to be with the Lord, to dwell in the shelter of his tent, to see his face, to live in the house of the Lord 'all the days of my life'. 'Though father and mother forsake me' (v. 10) is very forceful. The intensity of God's love is often compared to a father's or a mother's love, and we must remember that this is in a Jewish context, where a united and loving family is of paramount importance. Who can describe the emotional trauma of any mother abandoning her baby? And the parable of the prodigal son shows how Jesus sees the intensity of a father's love. That father and mother should both forsake a child is an unthinkable disaster, and yet the Lord will be there to receive me if that disaster should occur.

Corresponding to this warmth of relationship is the constant physical imagery of the psalm – gazing on the Lord's beauty, seeing the Lord's goodness, seeking the Lord's face, under the cover of his tent, within his tent. All of these phrases bespeak a sort of physical intimacy with the Lord.

Psalm 27[28]: To you, O Lord, I call

Here we are really confronted with the issue of the use of the Psalms! It is not easy to follow the sequence of thought in this psalm on the assumption that it is all spoken by one suppliant. If we take seriously the idea that the Psalms were all used for some part of the liturgy of the temple, we can divide this one into four sections, representing an interplay between two speakers:

Verses 1–5b: Individual lament, begging for release from persecution
Verse 5c: Reassurance pronounced by a representative of the temple
Verses 6–7: Praise and thanksgiving by the original suppliant
Verses 8–9: A final, more general blessing by the representative of the temple

The main speaker of the psalm could be the king or the high priest, for only these two are anointed, and 'his Anointed' (v. 8b) is in the singular. There is a strong parallel to 'his people' (v. 8a). No doubt, if the anointed king finds salvation in the Lord's stronghold, the people will also be saved.

With regard to the pleas for vengeance, this is a psalm where the Christian must principally rejoice in the progress of revelation. The straightforward reliance on God is touching, but Christian spirituality surpasses that of the psalm on three points. Firstly, the finality of going down into 'the pit' (v. 1) no longer obtains: for the Christian, death is not a blank ending, a descent into the grim world of Sheol, but a door through which we all pass towards eternal life. Secondly, the thirst for payback and vengeance (vv. 4–5) is not part of a Christian attitude, since Jesus taught so repeatedly that there is no place for revenge but only for the joy of forgiveness, for not only 'vertically' receiving the forgiveness of God but also for 'horizontally' sharing it with others. Thirdly, the Lord is indeed a saving refuge for his anointed (v. 8), since he vindicated and exalted his Anointed One, Jesus, and with Jesus takes up all his anointed ones who share in the body of Christ.

Psalm 28[29]: Ascribe to the Lord glory and strength!

This noble psalm in praise of God is built on a sharp contrast. It begins and ends (vv. 1–2, 10–11) with the calm of heaven, where the 'heavenly powers' (themselves gods and goddesses of myth) reverence the Lord. Within this envelope comes the turmoil on earth provoked by the Lord's powerful action. It is in the form of a victory song, like Miriam's victory song in the exodus after the crossing of the Reed Sea (Exodus 15:1–18), celebrating the Lord's strength and the glory of his name (v. 2).

Several features of the psalm are drawn from the Canaanite culture that Israel found on entering the promised land. The rhythm is characteristic of Canaanite poetry. Three times occurs the figure, typical of Canaanite poetry, consisting of two lines parallel with a third element added (1, 2 // 1, 2, *3*). So we have 'The Lord's voice on the waters, the Lord on the waters *in quantity*' (v. 3), then 'The Lord's voice shatters the cedars, the Lord shatters the cedars *of Lebanon*' (v. 5), and finally 'The Lord's voice shakes the wilderness, the Lord shakes the wilderness *of Kadesh*' (v. 8). The most powerful things in nature are shattered. The Israelites were daunted by the sea and pictured it as an uncontrollable sea-monster. The majestic cedars of Lebanon tower and spread in their might. The huge Mount Hermon ('Sirion' is the Phoenician name) is made to heave and bound. The Greek version of verse 6b reads 'like a young rhinoceros' instead of 'like a young wild ox', and it is hard to think of anything in the animal kingdom less bouncy than a rhinoceros. The Lord, meanwhile, sits majestically enthroned over the flood (v. 10), which, in local mythology, was another goddess of the chaotic and dreaded sea.

It is possible that this psalm was originally a Canaanite prayer addressed to their god, Baal, and that it was simply taken over, with the substitution of the name 'the Lord' for 'Baal'. Baal was a storm-god who made his presence and power known in storm and lightning; he was often represented as standing on a bull and hurling a thunderbolt. As we have already seen, the visitation of the Lord is often described in the Bible in similar terms of thunder and earthquake, derived from Israel's experience of the Lord on Sinai and in the wilderness of Kadesh. In this psalm there is the same turmoil in nature, but provoked by the more majestic and intangible voice of the Lord, which strikes seven times (the number of perfection) in the course of the psalm. From his throne the Lord effortlessly controls nature and gives strength and power to his people.

Psalm 29[30]: I will thank you, Lord, for you have drawn me up

In this psalm, the title is verse 1.

This is an attractive little prayer of thanksgiving for rescue from death. The thanks of the first three verses set the scene. All other biblical instances of the word translated 'drawn me up' are of water drawn up in a bucket from a well or a river: the psalmist has been drawn up like water from a well. This also fits the idea of being lifted from Sheol or the pit, for, until the idea of resurrection life became clear, death was envisaged as the descent into a grim and powerless half-life among similar shades. One had no strength there even to praise the Lord! At the arrival of the king of Babylon, the shades would rise up from the powerlessness of their thrones, only to sink back down again into their impotence (Isaiah 14:9–11).

In the main part of the psalm (bracketed by 'sing psalms' and 'thanks' in both verses 5 and 13), the psalmist does not explain in what the threat of death consisted. He only makes clear that his complacent self-confidence in being 'like a mountain fastness' was shattered, replaced by a helpless plea for the Lord's loving mercy. He seems almost to have challenged the Lord: 'Can dust give you praise or proclaim your faithfulness?' (v. 10). Was this a military, a moral or a medical crisis? At any rate, there was a pretty sharp conversion from self-reliance to reliance on the Lord, expressed in the sackcloth of repentance.

It is difficult to envisage the circumstances of the original use of this psalm in the temple. Later tradition associates it with thanksgiving for the deliverance of the temple from desecration at the time of the Maccabean persecution (167–164BC). Whatever the original circumstances, the frank, personal and joyful tone makes it a lovely prayer for any occasion when one's own self-assurance, mental, physical or moral, has been stripped away and one is forced to throw oneself cheerfully on to the mercy of God's own bucket-lift.

Psalm 30[31]: In you, O Lord, I take refuge

In this psalm, the title is verse 1.

This lament is puzzling, with two puzzles in particular. The first is that it seems to be a tissue of sentiments that occur elsewhere in the Bible (including the Psalms). Commentators call these 'conventional formulae'. It is as though the composer of the psalm, not wanting to use his own language, had culled them elsewhere and brought them all together. Rather than listing all the 'conventional formulae', I simply draw attention to the close similarity between the first two verses and the opening of Psalm 70[71], and between verse 14 and Jeremiah 20:10. Most of the other instances could be explained as merely the conventional language and imagery of distress.

The second puzzle concerns the sudden change from lament to thanksgiving, and arises from our ignorance of the liturgical context and use of the psalms. Ought we to assume a certain amount of action in the background to the texts? Is a liturgical procession for the entry of the ark into the temple the background of Psalm 23[24]? In Psalm 27[28], is there a real dialogue between a suppliant and a representative of the temple? In our present psalm (and correspondingly in others), should we assume the intervention of a blessing after verse 19, which turns the suppliant from lament to thanksgiving?

The structure of the first part of the psalm may be understood as a chiasmus, or Chinese box pattern:

Verses 2–6: Confident prayer for help
    Verses 7–9: Declaration of trust in the Lord
        Verses 10–14: Lament
    Verses 15–16: Declaration of trust in the Lord
Verses 17–19: Confident prayer for deliverance

This is followed by the thanks and praise of verses 20–25.

One precious feature is verse 6, placed by Luke (23:46) as Jesus' last words on the cross. Mark 15:34 and Matthew 27:46 give the intonation of Psalm 21[22], implying that the message of the triumph of God and the vindication of the sufferer is the lesson of that whole dire scene. The gospel of John has a very different episode (19:26–27), in which Jesus founds the first Christian community by joining together Mary and the beloved disciple, upon whom he breathes forth his Spirit.

Luke's interpretation brings to a close the great scene in which Jesus concludes his whole mission of bringing God's forgiveness to the world. He forgives his executioners and welcomes the repentant 'thief' into his kingdom. After that, he himself voluntarily entrusts his life to his Father, and the scene ends with the general repentance of the bystanders. Such a peaceful ending to a tumultuous and galling story would have been much valued by the Hellenistic audiences for whom Luke wrote: in Hellenistic literature it was considered important that a story should come to rest in tranquillity.

Psalm 31[32]: Blessed the sinner whose offence is forgiven

This was St Augustine's favourite psalm. As he lay dying, he had it written on the wall where he could see it and reflect upon it for encouragement. Like all psalms that begin with the promise 'Blessed is…', it has a Wisdom element, but the dominant characteristic is joy in the frank confession of sin.

The first part (vv. 3–5) lays out the story of guilt. At first I pretend that nothing is wrong. I hide my guilt even from myself, almost convincing myself. But the discomfort and strain become too great, and I may recognise that the firm hand of God is pressing upon me till I can no longer evade the pressure. As soon as I decide to acknowledge my sin ('I will confess' – future), the guilt has already (past tense) been forgiven. God demands no long or tortuous process. That was how Jesus went out to tax collectors, sinners, prostitutes, scribes and Pharisees, and drew them into God's forgiveness, not conditionally on their first changing their ways or even promising to amend. Jesus did not interrogate the sinful woman who anointed him about her intentions (Luke 7:36–51). 'I am to stay at your house today,' he said to Zacchaeus when Zacchaeus had shown only curiosity, not repentance (Luke 19:1–5). It is enough that I should respond to the touch of God's hand by admitting that I am myself the real source of the trouble. Immediately God becomes a hiding-place, a place of safety and refuge, 'with cries of deliverance' (v. 7).

After this personal and intimate self-revelation, there follows a short didactic section in a different rhythm and the imaged Wisdom style (vv. 8–10), using the lively figure of harnessing a stubborn mount. It is difficult to know who the speaker and the recipient, the 'I' and the 'you', are. Is God assuring the repentant sinner of continued guidance, or is the latter sharing what he has learnt with others? The warmth and tenderness of the previous section is continued in the idea of being surrounded by God's loving mercy, linked back to being surrounded by cries of deliverance (v. 7). Finally the psalmist simply breaks out into cries of joy.

Psalm 32[33]: The word of the Lord

In the first three verses, this psalm is firmly established as a song of joyful triumph. The last word of verse 3 clinches it: *teru'ah* means a fanfare or battle cry, an acclamation or cry of victory – in any case, noisy and celebratory. What is being celebrated?

The next part of the psalm (vv. 4–12) celebrates the creation, how the world was brought into being by the word of the Lord. The last part (vv. 13–22) concentrates on the Lord's continuing oversight of human affairs, as he watches or gazes on the world and we wait for the final revelation of his faithful love. Any possibility that the Lord is a mere control-freak is excluded by this envelope of the concept of faithful love (vv. 5, 22). On the contrary, God's direction of the world is an expression of his faithful and fatherly love for his people, that brilliant word *hesed*, which designates the unbreakable reciprocal love of family members towards one another. This is the unfailing love that God has promised to his people.

The first part of this triumphant celebration dwells on the creation narrative, where God 'spoke and it came into being', circling round three concepts: the spreading out of the heavens (v. 6), the gathering together of the waters (v. 7), and the firm establishment of the earth and its peoples (v. 8). God's design is supreme and unalterable. For the Christian, this whole idea is enriched and reaches its fullness by the designation of Jesus as the incarnate Word of God (John 1:1–18), who brings creation to its completion and in whom creation reaches its zenith (Ephesians 1:10, the climax of the great hymn of God's plan). Christ is the *logos* of God's design, the master-plan personified, who gives sense, order and direction to the whole of creation.

The celebration is not, however, confined to the act of creation in the 'Big Bang' eons ago, for the second half of the psalm relates to God's continuing work of creation as he watches over the world. No king and his army, no horse and its strength (note the neat parallels of verses 16 and 17) can disturb God's designs. All is directed towards the outworking of God's *hesed* for his people (vv. 18, 22), and issues in the same joy with which the psalm began. The final mention of 'waiting for the Lord' (v. 20) directs Christian attention to the prophecy of the eschatological city of God, the new Jerusalem (Revelation 21—22), the final consummation for which we are waiting.

Psalm 33[34]: Taste and see that the Lord is good

In this psalm, the title is verse 1.

This is an acrostic psalm in the Wisdom tradition, and its formal data are easily summarised. Each verse begins with a successive letter of the Hebrew alphabet (only one being omitted, and one verse added at the end of the series), which gives the psalm a certain, not unpleasant, stiffness of expression. The parallelism of the pairs of lines is very pronounced, sometimes in the same direction (for example, v. 4), sometimes in opposite directions (for example, v. 10). After the extended and joyful invitation to praise the Lord (vv. 2–9), the didactic or Wisdom part begins, gently giving rules for good conduct.

The chief burden of the teaching is to revere or fear the Lord (vv. 8, 10, 12). Fear and reverence are not particularly modern virtues. In a person-to-person society, we pride ourselves on standing tall and independent from anyone, not cringing before any potentate or authority. Precisely! God is not anyone. By no stretch of the imagination can we stand proud before God. In a wonderful poem, Isaiah describes the only due reaction to God: 'Go into the rock, hide in the dust, in terror of the Lord, at the brilliance of his majesty, when he arises to make the earth quake' (Isaiah 2:10). This is why the sacred/scary intimate name of the Lord, YHWH, is never pronounced. In his vocation experience of the Lord in the temple, Isaiah cringes as unclean before the Holy One of Israel (6:5). St Augustine describes his awe before this daunting presence: '*inhorresco et inardesco*', 'I burn with longing, but the hairs on the nape of my neck stand on end' (*Confessions*, II.9.1).'Perfect love drives out fear,' we are told (1 John 4:18), but only one sort of fear, and we must never lose our awed reverence at our incomparability to God.

The optimism of the moral teaching of this psalm may seem excessive at a surface level. The Christian believes that the Lord will eventually rescue the righteous from all their distress (v. 18), but not necessarily in this world. It is a hope that sustains us in the long run. However, there are times when we find that Job's anger and protests at his inexplicable suffering chime in more fittingly with our own feelings. We cannot understand why we should suffer so much while the wicked get off scot-free. This is where Job's awe at his final experience of the wisdom and power of the Lord comes in. We cannot question God's plan; we can only accept it in consciousness of our own limitations.

Psalm 34[35]: Take up your buckler and shield

In reflecting on this psalm, asking for strength and victory against opponents, the first question to ask is what sort of opponents are envisaged. There is plenty of military language – buckler, shield, javelin, spear – but there is also other imagery: the opponents are like lions; they are to be like chaff in the wind, their path a slippery slope. The predominant imagery is, however, of the law courts. The opening plea is expressed in terms of strife at law, and ideas compatible with this recur constantly: lying witnesses, asking questions, shame, mockery, vindication and disgrace, rather than wounds, blood and death. Military imagery can be more easily used in a legal situation than legal imagery in a military situation. The betrayal by the friend whom the psalmist supported during sickness (vv. 12–14) also fits this legal scene better.

For the purposes of our own prayer, however, an appeal for justice in the law courts is of little use. We know only too well that, in many ways, we are far from innocent before the Lord. Personally I find little appeal in the solution of imagining the enemies as devils or temptations: it is too easy to personify in this way my own evil tendencies, as though they, and not I, were responsible for my frequent failures. I prefer, therefore, to concentrate on, and pray about, the concepts of divine justice and salvation.

In ordinary language, if I cry out for justice, I want to set right something that is wrong. Someone who is 'brought to justice' is normally punished. When 'justice is done', it can have overtones of vengeance. Justice occurs in the function of law. In the Bible, also, justice is in the function of law, but it is God's Law, given to Israel, and this makes a total difference. God's Law is God's revelation, enabling us to imitate God, to live as the image of God and in harmony with God. It is the furtherance of the promises to Abraham that God would protect him and make his offspring like the sand on the seashore. So it is a saving justice, in accord with God's saving generosity, not giving us our deserved punishment but precisely rescuing us from our deserts. So Isaiah can say of God, 'My saving justice will last forever and my salvation for all generations' (51:8). In the same way, Paul can appeal to God's saving justice (sometimes translated 'righteousness'). We are rescued from punishment by God's saving justice, simply by trusting in that saving justice.

Psalm 35[36]: Your mercy, O Lord, reaches to heaven

In this psalm, the title is verse 1.

This psalm is often contrasted with Psalm 1, which characterises first the friend of God (like a well-watered tree) and then the evildoer (like chaff before the wind). This psalm does somewhat the same in reverse, first reflecting on the complacent and godless evildoer ('his words are mischief and deceit', v. 4), then rejoicing in God's generous mercy ('in your light we see light', v. 10). Verses 6–11 are more a celebration of God's mercy than a prayer for it, though such a prayer is of course implied.

However, this celebration of God's mercy provokes us to continue the reflections of the previous psalm on God's saving justice, since God's righteousness and his mercy are strongly similar concepts. In the central section, God's mercy is mentioned three times, God's justice or righteousness twice, and God's truth or fidelity also. After the first breaking of the covenant on Mount Sinai, God's nature, the meaning of the divine name YHWH, was revealed to Moses as mercy and forgiveness (Exodus 34:6–7); so these three concepts circle round the same idea. God is true to the divine nature and to the divine Law revealed on Sinai precisely by being merciful and by forgiving. For us sinners, therefore, this is life and light: 'in your light we see light'. The friend of God is not so much the person who acts blamelessly as one who turns to God and puts all trust in the divine forgiveness.

Such an attitude may well produce the occasional good action, too! As the letter of James challenges, 'So you have faith and I have good deeds? Show me this faith of yours without deeds, then! It is by my deeds that I will show you my faith' (2:18). However, the difference between the evildoer and the friend of God consists in the attitude: really determined evildoers are satisfied and complacent in their own plots and self-absorption, whereas those 'of upright heart' put all their trust outside themselves, in God's mercy, forgiveness and saving justice.

Psalm 36[37]: Do not fret because of the wicked

This is a fine example of a Wisdom psalm, built on an alphabetical framework. In the Hebrew, the structure is quite regular, each pair of lines beginning with a successive letter of the alphabet. In the translation, nearly all of these pairs come out as a quatrain, though occasionally in three or five lines. As a Wisdom psalm, it is built on the conventional Hebrew teaching that the moral life brings its own reward – in the end. God rewards those who are faithful to him and his teachings.

But does he? This simplistic morality seems to be built on a system of rewards and punishments in this life. Does honesty really pay? Practical experience teaches that this is not, in fact, the case. There are enough successful sharks around to call into question the comfortable assertion, 'A little longer and the wicked one is gone' (v. 10). The Bible itself questions this teaching massively in the book of Job, where Job doggedly retains his loyalty to God even though he feels himself hounded and tortured by God. No less, the book of Qoheleth (Ecclesiastes) questions all the assumptions about happiness in this life. What, then, of the simple morality of the Beatitudes, which echoes so many verses here? 'The humble shall own the land' (v. 11; Matthew 5:4)? They don't. Must we rely on pie in the sky as a reward for drudgery in this life?

No Christian who prays this psalm can limit the prayer to such bargain-morality. Nor does this psalm itself. Such a relationship to God would be about as successful as a marriage undertaken so that each partner could get as much as possible out of the other. Our relationship to God must be one of getting to know the Lord more and more profoundly and intimately, and being more and more ready to sacrifice ourselves for the beloved. If there is love, a mother delights in the chores of motherhood, and spouse delights in caring for spouse. Lovers will put up with anything as long as they can stay together. The most wearisome or demeaning task undertaken for the beloved becomes a joy. So in the psalm there is a companionship and love that goes beyond a mere bargain: 'Be still before the Lord and wait in patience' (v. 7). The only factor that counts is joy in the relationship. If truly 'the Law of God is in his heart' (v. 31), then prosperity and adversity take second place.

Psalm 37[38]: Lord, do not correct me in anger

In this psalm, the title is verse 1.

This is a strange and touching psalm. The psalmist makes use of an extraordinarily rich and varied vocabulary, in both words and images, to describe his unenviable situation. The Lord's arrows, his hand and his indignation are all against him. Sin reaches higher than his head. He endures stinking, festering wounds, deafness and dumbness, desertion by his friends and unprovoked opposition from those who hate him. Such a rich cornucopia of horrors simultaneously cannot be meant literally.

Touchingly, the psalmist makes no secret of his own sin, mentioning it in verses 4 and 19 but without making a meal of it. So matter-of-fact is he about his sin that he makes no protestations of innocence (as we find so often in the psalms). The psalm is numbered among the traditional seven penitential psalms – the others being 6, 30[31], 50[51], 100[101], 128[129] and 141[142] – but there is no litany of repentance. The psalmist stands before the Lord guilty and unashamed. Certainly there is no whisper of exaggerated or hypocritical bewailing of sin.

When this is combined with the two pleas with which the psalm begins and ends, there is something noble and very attractive about such realism. If we remember that Jesus did not go out to find those who were already repentant and had given up their evil ways, but went out to find sinners and 'compel them to come in' to the great banquet, we can imagine that this psalmist would have been quick to respond. If I had to place the psalm on the lips of any New Testament character, I would offer it to the woman taken in adultery. Was she praying it as she stood before Jesus?

One matter deserves special attention: verse 12b gives us literally, 'My nearest ones keep at a distance.' This juxtaposition of exact opposites expresses utter betrayal by those most intimate and dear. The verse comes by allusion in the passion narrative (Mark 15:40), where the women are watching 'at a distance'. A number of the details of the passion of Jesus are carefully presented in such a way as to show the detailed fulfilment of scripture. Of course, the passion of Jesus fulfilled the whole of scripture and the will and intentions of the Father, but the authors of the sacred texts picked out individual texts to show how this was so. We may feel that the women are unfairly treated by this allusion. It was, after all, the betrayal by Judas, after sharing Jesus' own dish, that was the ultimate desertion. The women did at least stick near him to the end, which is more than can be said of the men.

Psalm 38[39]: I will watch how I behave

In this psalm, the title is verse 1.

This psalm is a lovely reflection on the insubstantiality of human life and existence. The images are repeated: a 'puff of wind' (vv. 6, 7, 12), a mere 'shadow' (v. 7), my days a couple of 'hand's breadths' (v. 6). I am a 'foreigner', an 'alien' with no rights of residence (v. 13), even though, in the Law, immigrants were to be treated with special consideration, precisely because they were so helpless. In the end, the psalmist requests time for a brief smile and then simply walks off the stage, so to speak, and is no more, ceases to exist (v. 14).

There is, in addition, a consciousness of sin, of the need for self-restraint and of the reality of deserved punishment, but these elements are not so prominent. Reliance on and a touching confidence in the Lord are complete (v. 8). Standing in overwhelming contrast to the insubstantiality of human existence is the solidity of the Lord, who sets the length of life (v. 5) and can punish or correct at will (v. 12).

How does all this fit with what we know of God from Christian revelation? The most touching aspect of the poem is the complete confidence in the Lord, without any hint of a promise of eternal life or any kind of life after death. The psalmist does not seem to yearn for a reward after death or for eternal company with the Lord. Nor, for that matter, is there any mention of the grim, insubstantial half-life in Sheol, where it is impossible even to praise God. In our poem, the psalmist is safe in God's hands, without any look to a possible future.

I would suggest that the aspect of this psalm that we should treasure is the readiness for a revelation of life after death. The stage is set for this revelation, which seems to have come with the martyrdoms of the Maccabean persecution in the early second century BC. The ground was prepared, as we can see in many of the psalms – a sure indication of Israel's prayer life and beliefs – by the conviction that God's loving care for every individual is so unbreakable that it must transcend death. As Jesus would show in his reply to the Sadducees (Matthew 22:32), the God of Abraham, Isaac and Jacob is a God of the living, not of the dead.

Psalm 39[40]: You do not ask for sacrifice… but an open ear

In this psalm, the title is verse 1.

This psalm falls into three parts, each of which might exist or might have existed independently:

- Verses 2–6: Praise of God and thanksgiving for an answer to prayer
- Verses 7–12: A reflection, in the manner of the prophets, on the relative value of sacrifice and obedience
- Verses 13–18: A plea for rescue from some hostile threat

To the Christian, the central section must appeal most, for it is used in the letter to the Hebrews to interpret the value of Christ's sacrifice. The prophet Samuel had already reproached and rejected Saul (somewhat unfairly, it seems to me) for offering a sacrifice instead of waiting for Samuel himself to arrive and make the offering (1 Samuel 13:8–14). The later prophets constantly stress that a sacrifice which does not express submission to and love of God is hypocritical and vain. This idea is repeated in an absolute form in verse 7. Hebrew thinking is frequently absolute in a way that seems overemphatic; so Jesus teaches that love of him must triumph even over love of family, saying, 'You must hate father and mother' (see Luke 14:26). Similarly, this psalm teaches that obedience is more important than sacrifice, not that sacrifice and offering have no purpose.

Hebrews 10:1-10 uses this text to contrast the saving efficacy of the obedience of Jesus with the sacrificial blood of bulls and goats. The crucifixion was the supreme act of human obedience. Adam's disobedience is not the story of what happened to one man at the beginning of the human race; it is the story of human disobedience as such, repeated down the centuries. 'Adam' means 'man', as we have seen, and the story of the Fall is the story of human falling, as it occurs again and again. By his obedience, which was human but more than human, Jesus undid this disobedience. By his highest act of love to his Father, he transcended the human lack of love for God. There can be no question of Jesus being separated from his Father at that time; it was the most complete possible act of union to the Father, in which the human race was restored to peace with God, restored to oneness with God. It was not the blood of Christ, any more than the blood of bulls and goats, that 'saved' us. We use the word only as an image to represent the loving obedience of Jesus, even to the point of death – to the point of shedding his blood.

Psalm 40[41]: Blessed is one who has concern for the poor

In this psalm, the title is verse 1.

The most notable feature of this psalm is its positioning. The detached final verse, a doxology or verse of praise to God, marks the end of the first 'book' of psalms, for each of the five 'books' of psalms so ends (71[72]:19; 88[89]:52; [105]106:48; 150). It acts as a closing bracket to the book, for its form balances Psalm 1: both begin with the announcement of a blessing on a particular kind of activity. The first section is typical of Wisdom psalms, such as Psalm 1. This psalm is a particularly important act of faith, since so many of the psalms within these brackets voice complaints that the Lord does not, in fact, always bless those who attend to the poor and the weak!

The storyline of the psalm is prayer in time of sickness. It begins with a firm assertion of confidence in constant divine care for the faithful sick (vv. 2–5a), which ends, 'Lord, have mercy on me.' It finishes with a prayer that the Lord will repeat this favour for the psalmist himself (vv. 11–13), and this prayer begins, 'Lord, have mercy on me', again a neat little balance.

Between the assertion and the prayer is a heartfelt but slightly humorous presentation of a series of visitors to the sick person, all of whom are in fact gloating over the sufferer. The first just can't wait till the sick man dies. The second speaks soothing words but changes his tune to malicious rumour the moment he leaves the bedside. A third – this time a group of visitors – simply gather in a corner and decide with satisfaction that there is no chance of recovery. Beware, hospital visitors: better stay away than give rise to such suspicions!

For the Christian echoes of the psalm, we must turn again to the passion narrative. If the psalm is thought of as being written by David, the trusted friend is often cast as Ahithophel, the counsellor who betrayed David by going over to Absalom and then committed suicide. His death foreshadows that of Judas in Matthew 27:5. Verse 10 of our psalm is quoted in the Johannine account of the last supper (John 13:18) to illustrate the depths of the traitor's treachery. In the Near East, hospitality still creates a sacred bond, so that to offer or accept hospitality (even a glass of water) is a serious matter. 'One who has eaten my bread' can never stand in a casual relationship to me again. Whatever is meant by 'has lifted his heel against me', the principal agony in this case is the denial of a bond of committed mutual obligation.

Book 2

Psalm 41—42[42—43]: Like the deer that yearns for running streams

In this psalm, the title is verse 1.

These two psalms are often considered to be a single psalm, and rightly so. They both end with the same quatrain, binding them together. Another repeated refrain-like verse is found at 41[42]:10 and 42[43]:2. So it will here be assumed that this was originally a single psalm, later divided into two for some liturgical purpose.

For many people, the psalm makes a favourite prayer, as an expression of the ardent longing to come close to God. The psalmist appears to be distanced from God and longing to 'see the face' of God in the temple (41[42]:3). The imagery is of the far north of the country, the foothills of Mount Hermon, where the River Jordan rises (v. 7). The location of the Hill of Mizar is unknown, but the expression means no more than 'the insignificant hill'.

The lovely opening line conjures up the many little sparkling streams in the foothills of Hermon, which flow into the swelling stream of the Jordan. The roar of the torrents (v. 8) evokes the thunderous waterfall of the Jordan, just below Caesarea Philippi. From there, the 'wondrous tent' and ceremonies of Jerusalem, the throng keeping joyful festival (41[42]:5), the holy mountain and the altar of God (42[43]:3-4) seem a world away, a distant nirvana.

By his transfer of the ark to Jerusalem, David had made Jerusalem not only his own capital but also the Lord's dwelling place. At Solomon's dedication of the temple, the Lord had dramatically taken possession of it (1 Kings 8:10-11). In the sanctuary, filled with the train of the Lord, Isaiah had experienced his prophetic call (Isaiah 6). The ultimate disaster of the exile was the departure from the temple of God's glory (Ezekiel 11:23), and the ultimate promise of forgiveness was the return of the glory of the Lord to the rebuilt temple (Ezekiel 43:5). Here was the place to 'see the face' of God, to enter into the divine presence.

The intensity of the psalmist's longing is conveyed by the sevenfold 'my soul'. In Hebrew, the soul is not detachable from the body, to be breathed out at one's last gasp. It designates a person's whole being, so 'my soul yearns' expresses an intensely personal and wholehearted yearning. In the related Aramaic, the word *nefesh* is used for the reflexive: 'I pour out my soul' means 'I pour my whole self out.' Jesus' saying in Mark 8:36 means, 'What does it profit one to gain the whole world and lose oneself?' So the seven mentions of 'my soul' express the passionate intensity of the longing for the presence of the Lord.

Psalm 43[44]: We heard with our own ears, O God

In this psalm, the title is verse 1.

This may be considered the first of the historical psalms, and also the first of the corporate laments. The psalmist is puzzled by the failure of the Lord to protect his own: the shepherd of Israel, instead of caring for his sheep and fattening them up, has yielded them up for slaughter (vv. 12, 23).

The structure of the psalm says it all:

- Verses 2–4: God's unfailing protection in times past. According to the conventional biblical account in the book of Joshua (partly modified in Judges 1), God drove out nations to make room for Israel.
- Verses 5–9: Protestations of the psalmist's sturdy trust in God for protection. Israel has always relied for protection on God, never on its own strength.

- Verses 10–17: God's desertion of his own people, leaving them to be defeated, mocked and taunted by neighbouring nations.
- Verses 18–23: Protestations of innocence. The psalmist is well aware that infidelity to God would merit such punishment as a corrective, but protests that the nation has remained wholly faithful. Despite this, the sheep are being slaughtered for the sake of the shepherd.
- Verses 24–27: A plea to God to awake and remedy the situation, finally calling on God's *hesed*.

The date of the psalm is impossible to establish. It can hardly be referring to the time of the Babylonian exile, for at that time Israelites were acutely conscious that their infidelity was responsible for their defeats and exile. A hint that the psalm referred to the Maccabean persecution is the story in the Talmud that every day a Levite was appointed to cry out in the temple, 'It is for you we are slain all day long' (v. 23), a practice that was ended by King John Hyrcanus (134–104BC), by which time Jerusalem was again freed from persecution. The psalm would indeed be appropriate to that period, for the persecution of the Jews by King Antiochus was aimed precisely at destroying their fidelity to the Law, and the psalm proclaims their stubborn fidelity.

The puzzlement is well focused by ending the psalm on the word *hesed*, the covenant-love of God for Israel. In a passage that echoes through the scriptures, God had revealed himself to Moses, at the moment of Israel's first great betrayal, as a 'God of tenderness and compassion, slow to anger, rich in faithful love (*hesed*) and constancy' (Exodus 34:6). By contrast, Israel's *hesed* for God passes 'like morning mist' (Hosea 6:4). God's loyalty to Israel is inextinguishable. It was promised to Abraham, to David and to his dynasty. Most of all, it was the everlasting love that the Lord had promised to Israel, his spouse (Isaiah 54.8). How, then, could it fail?

Psalm 44[45]: My heart overflows with noble words

In this psalm, the title is verse 1.

This psalm is unique in the psalter, being addressed not to God but to a human couple. It is described in its heading as a love song. We can no longer establish for which royal wedding it was composed. One possibility is the wedding of King Ahab to Jezebel, the daughter of the priest-king of Tyre (v. 12). The 'ivory palace' (v. 8) would also fit this setting, for Amos complains of the ivory decorations in the palaces at Samaria.

As a royal wedding song, it is obviously very formal, dwelling on the military prowess of the king as well as the justice and clemency of his rule, on the distinction and retinue of his bride as well as her beauty. There is hardly a mention of God, so why is it included in the psalter? One possible answer is that the king is always God's representative, but a more satisfactory answer is the messianic interpretation that was attached to it once the Judean monarchy had come to an end. The compliments paid to the king are elaborate enough to make him a sort of ideal and universal king of fidelity and righteousness, for the 'wondrous deeds' (v. 4) evoke the wonders of the messianic time described in Isaiah 35. The repeated stress on the eternal endurance of the king's reign (vv. 2c, 6) is reminiscent of the promises to the eternal priest-king in Psalm 110.

Verse 6 yields a particular richness. 'Your throne shall endure forever' can be read as a prediction of eternity – either of the personal reign or of the dynasty. However, Hebrews 1:8 uses this verse to show the divinity of Christ, one of the very few passages in the New Testament to affirm it directly. This is, no doubt, building on a contemporary understanding of the dignity of the Messiah, in whom God is seen to be at work. The original Hebrew is awkward: what has God's throne ('Your throne, O God') to do here? The idea of God's throne is introduced quite suddenly, and this verse is the only place in the psalm addressing God directly; it has neither preparation nor follow-up. The verse could be interpreted, 'God is your throne forever' – that is, the basis of your rule. Alternatively, the word 'O God' has been frequently emended to 'like God' or simply 'shall', both minor changes of a letter or two. Whatever the original author sang or meant, this verse forms an important basis of the christological argument of Hebrews.

Psalm 45[46]: God is for us a refuge and strength

In this psalm, the title is verse 1.

This neat psalm falls into three three-verse sections, with a refrain after each (at least, after the second and third sections, so it is usually supplied after the first). The first section celebrates God's sure help during the natural turmoil of earthquake, the third celebrates God's sure help in times of military threat, and the second celebrates the peace of the city where God dwells.

Verses 2–4 envisage cosmic turmoil. The Hebrew concept of the universe was of a terrifyingly powerful churning mass of waters. God divided the waters and settled the flat earth on pillars, at the same time holding off the waters above by means of the dome of the heavens. If it were not for God's continuous restraint, the mass of waters could at any moment engulf and obliterate the world as we know it. Against this ever-present threat, and its partial reality in the devastation of earthquake, God is the only security. God's act of creation – or of non-obliteration – is continuous.

Verses 5–7 turn lovingly towards Jerusalem, peaceful and well-watered by the plentiful Spring of Gihon. Day breaks in Jerusalem when the sun rises serenely over the Mount of Olives to the east. There is no need to restrict the meaning to some particular day, for the divine protection is absolute and sure. In this section of the psalter, the personal divine name, 'the Lord', the affectionate family name, too holy and too intimate to be pronounced, occurs rarely. Its use here is perhaps provoked by the intimacy of the divine presence in Jerusalem. At the same time, it is combined with the majestic and mythical title 'Lord of hosts', probably referring to the hosts of heavenly powers, effortlessly controlled by God.

Verses 9–11 pit God's awesome power against conventional military might, which crumbles before him. This total ending of violence and oppression is an integral element in the reign of God to which the messianic promises look forward. For us, these verses must always stir consciences at the failure of Christians to implement this aspect of the kingship of God – indeed, at the persistence of wars of religion over the centuries and even inter-Christian divisions and hostility. The instruction 'Be still and know that I am God' (v. 11) does not necessarily refer primarily to the tranquillity of contemplative prayer, for prayer in Israel was a noisy and celebratory affair. Rather, it signifies that the power of God is such that we can relax and merely admire that power at work.

Psalm 46[47]: All peoples, clap your hands!

In this psalm, the title is verse 1.

This is the first of a number of psalms celebrating the kingship of the Lord. Even in Israel's post-monarchical, post-exilic days, kingship was a powerful metaphor for the highest and most awesome exaltation, denoting unlimited authority over subjects and an obligation to be alert to their needs and to care for them. God is our Father, but also our Master. With so much clapping, shouting and the fivefold 'Sing praise', it is obviously a psalm of unbridled celebration.

This psalm is in the classic form of a song of praise: an invitation to praise, followed by the reason for so doing. The formula is twice repeated, the first reason (vv. 3–5) being the Lord's defeat of the various tribes in Canaan to win a heritage for Israel, and the second (vv. 8–10) the homage paid by all nations to Israel's God. This second element is what may indicate a post-exilic date. It was only by confrontation with the multiple divine figures of Babylon that Israel came to realise that the Lord, their God, was sovereign not only of Israel but of all nations. From then onwards, Israel began to see that all nations would come to draw salvation from Zion, a theme of increasing importance in Israel's post-exilic worldview.

In the early 20th century, the Scandinavian scholar Sigmund Mowinkel popularised the theory that Israel celebrated an annual new year festival of the kingship of God, in which God was ceremonially re-enthroned in the temple. 'The Lord is king' can also be translated, 'The Lord has become king', as though God had notionally ceased to be king or had been re-enthroned. There is evidence for such a festival in other Near Eastern cultures, but none for it in Israel. There is no trace of it in the full instructions in the Bible about worship and festivals. The theory has therefore waned. The words 'The Lord goes up with trumpet blast' (v. 6) may be understood to signify not such an annual procession but either Israel going up into the hill-country at the entry into Canaan, or a celebration of David taking the ark up into Jerusalem, by which Jerusalem was held to become the Lord's own dwelling-place on earth. In Christian thought, it is understood (by extension) to describe the risen Christ exalted at his resurrection and ascension to the right hand of God, as in Psalm 109[110].

Psalm 47[48]: Great is the Lord, and highly to be praised

In this psalm, the title is verse 1.

This psalm celebrating the Lord's protection of Jerusalem links with the previous two psalms, which celebrated respectively the peace at Jerusalem and the Lord's exaltation from Jerusalem. The presence of the Lord in his sanctuary at Jerusalem is the guarantee of the security and dignity of the city.

The first theme of praise seems to commemorate, in mythical terms, a military or naval victory. The terms are mythical because they veer between a gathering on land (the kings advancing, v. 5) and the ships of Tarshish. The east wind (v. 8) also has mythical significance, since it was the Lord's agent in shattering the enemy at the archetype of all victories, the crossing of the Red Sea. The east wind, lowering the water level, enabled the Hebrews to cross, and its cessation threw the pursuers into the sea. There is no indication of what military victory might be envisaged, and it is hard to see how Zion, a hilltop city on the central spine of the country, could be involved in a naval conflict. So perhaps the brunt of this theme is that Jerusalem is so well protected by the divine presence that it can weather any attack.

The second theme of praise is a walk around the city itself (vv. 13–14), an appreciative tour, in which the daughters of Judah rejoice and the towers, ramparts and castles impress by their number and strength. The cyclopean masonry of the ancient pre-Davidic walls of Jerusalem is still massively impressive, and enough remains of the post-exilic walls to show their strength as bastions. Apart from these, we know little of the architectural splendours of Jerusalem in the Old Testament period. Herod's magnificent temple, which made Jerusalem 'far the most distinguished city of the east' (according to Pliny), had yet to be built.

A couple of geographical features may puzzle us. How can Zion be described as 'in the heart of the north' (v. 3)? The word for 'north' is Zaphon, and the primitive gods of Canaan had their home primarily on the mountain Baal-Zaphon, in the north of Lebanon. It looks as though Zion, the dwelling place of God, has inherited this name as a sort of title. The other geographical feature, the 'ships of Tarshish', remains a puzzle. Tarshish itself has not been located, despite a variety of suggested locations, including Tartessos in far-off Spain. The description may also indicate the type of ship, a war ship or great merchant ship. It is best to give the expression the sense that it has also in modern English poetry – a magnificent galleon in full sail.

Psalm 48[49]: Hear this, all you people

In this psalm, the title is verse 1.

This psalm is shown especially by its introduction (vv. 2–5) to be a Wisdom psalm: all the language is about wisdom, listening, meditation, puzzling out. It does not invoke the Lord. It does not plead for anything or anyone. It is a reflection on the mysteries of life and death. Death is certain for rich as well as for poor. There is an inevitability about death, so there is no point in fearing life-threatening enemies (v. 6), and no point in thinking we can buy our way out of death with a high enough price (vv. 7–10). Nor will wisdom (vv. 11–12) or success (v. 19) postpone the evil day.

These reflections are summed up in the fierce and uncompromising refrain of verses 13 and 21, which puts human beings on a strict par with cattle being herded to slaughter. In the Greek version, these two verses are identical. In the Hebrew text, there is a witty little variation, built on a pun between *yalin* (v. 13) and *yabin* (v. 21). The former verb means 'camp/bivouac briefly for one night', so that we get literally 'by his wealth man does not get even to bivouac for one night' (v. 13) and 'by his wealth man does not get understanding' (v. 21).

At the time of this psalm, the Hebrew understanding of existence (we can hardly call it 'life') after death was grim in the extreme. The dead are confined to a subterranean life where they have no power or strength or any of the qualities that go to make up a real life. In Sheol you cannot praise God. The fullest accounts come in the mocking dirge over the king of Babylon in Isaiah 14:9–21 ('under you a mattress of maggots, over you a blanket of worms'), and in the recital of the hordes confined to oblivion in Ezekiel 32:11–32. Yet this psalm of ours has an unexplained and unexploited flicker of hope in verse 15, especially in the emphatic verse 16b, 'He will indeed receive me.' The belief in a real life after death was slow in coming, not reaching full expression till the martyrdoms of the Maccabean era. Yet the conviction was already there that God could not desert those who put their trust in him. It flickers also in Psalm 15[16]:10 and again in Psalm 72[73]:24, but above all in the splendid testimonial of Job 19:25–26, 'I know that I have a living Defender… and from my flesh I shall look on God.'

Psalm 49[50]: The God of Gods, the Lord, has spoken

In biblical times, the question of sacrifice arises again and again: what is its value, and what are the conditions for it? Is prayer a sufficient sacrifice or does God require animal sacrifices? There was always a danger of using sacrifice to avoid rather than to express genuine homage to God. The sayings of the earliest prophets, Amos and Hosea, denounce the hypocrisy of a sacrifice combined with fraud and oppression of God's favourites, the poor and needy. The present psalm mocks the absurd supposition that God actually needs animal sacrifice. It rejects sacrifice combined with disobedience to the word of God, with stealing, with adultery, deceit and slander. Perhaps most telling is the mocking question from God, 'Do you think that I am like you?' (v. 21). Sacrifice implies an affinity between the deity and the offerer, or at least an attempt to establish or strengthen such an affinity. Sacrifice must be an expression of homage and agreement of aims. But it is no use trying to pull God down to our level, or imagine a God with the same crookednesses as ourselves!

The psalm falls into three parts. It begins with the solemn entry of God on to the scene, almost the sun coming forth like a bridegroom coming from his tent (Psalm 18[19]:5). At the same time, God presents himself in awesome cosmic splendour and summons the whole earth to witness the judgment of his people (vv. 1-6). Such judgment scenes are familiar from the second part of Isaiah (43:8-13; 45:20-25), but none is so splendid as this.

Then God bears witness against the people of Israel (vv. 7-15). God does not reject their sacrifices out of hand but puts forward a better way – a sacrifice of praise. In the third part, God turns specifically to accuse the incorrigible wicked (vv. 16-22). God will tear them to pieces like a wild animal mangling its prey, and there will be no one to deliver them (v. 22). If God the Saviour is not there to deliver, this is terrible indeed! Finally, it is again repeated that a sacrifice of praise, rather than animal sacrifice, is what pleases God.

In the end, the sacrifice of praise is the most acceptable, and, towards the end of the Old Testament era, prayer comes to be regarded as a sacrifice of praise (for example, see the end of the next psalm). So, in Hebrews 5:7-8, Jesus' sacrifice is set out in terms of a prayer: 'During his life on earth, he offered up prayer and entreaty... to the one who had the power to save him... and, winning a hearing by his reverence, he learnt obedience, Son though he was, by his sufferings.' This prayer, too, was a sacrifice of praise.

Psalm 50[51]: Have mercy on me, O God

In this psalm, the title is verses 1–2.

This is the best-known and best-loved of the seven penitential psalms. The caption added later to the psalm associates it with David's repentance after his adultery with Bathsheba and his dastardly attempt to cover up his sin by bringing her husband Uriah home from the battlefield (and then having him killed). There is nothing in the psalm itself to attach it to this incident. Indeed, the final pair of verses reflects the period of the rebuilding of the temple after the return from exile, and the concern of that period about legitimate sacrifice. However, these two verses may well have been added, for the body of the psalm sets conversion above sacrifice.

The main body of the psalm falls into two halves, each in a chiasmus or Chinese-box pattern. It would be tedious to follow this out in detail, but the first half is bracketed by 'blot out... wash me... cleanse me' (vv. 3–4) and 'cleanse me... wash me... blot out' (vv. 9–11). It centres on confession of sin and awareness of inexcusable guilt: 'you are just in your sentence' (v. 6). The second half is bracketed by 'heart... spirit' (v. 12) and 'spirit... heart' (v. 19). It centres on God's salvation (vv. 14, 16) and the return of sinners. As the spirituality of the first half chimes in with the consciousness of sin and guilt in Jeremiah, so the second half is enriched by the teaching on a new heart and new spirit in the promises of Ezekiel. After the disastrous infidelities that led to the Babylonian exile, Israel will be endowed with a new heart – a heart of flesh instead of a heart of stone – and the spirit or breath of life (Ezekiel 36:26; 37:5). This is the joy of salvation, or the saving joy, which the psalmist will announce to sinners.

The real warmth of the psalm comes from the first three words. The opening word, translated 'Have mercy on me', is formed from the same word as for a mother's womb. It is a plea for the unbreakable love of a mother, which can never be denied to her children, whatever they may do – the affinity engendered by the mother carrying her baby for nine loving and expectant months in the womb. The third word, translated 'your merciful love' (yes, all one word in the Hebrew), appeals to the inviolable loyalty between members of the same family: I may find my brother difficult and obstinate, but, when push comes to shove, I won't let him down.

Psalm 51[52]: Why do you boast of wickedness?

In this psalm, the title is verses 1–2.

This is the first of three little psalms in which the psalmist is set against evil and powerful opponents. There is, however, no need to attach it to Doeg the Edomite, as the superscription does. Doeg betrayed David by telling Saul that David had purloined from the sanctuary the show-bread and Goliath's sword; but Doeg was a mere herdsman, not a champion (1 Samuel 21:1–10; 22:9–10).

The structure of this psalm falls neatly into three sections. The first (vv. 2–6) sharply and sarcastically badmouths the champion of evil. The second (vv. 7–9) shows us the righteous smugly and merrily laughing at the discomfiture and uprooting of this champion who trusted in his own prowess.

The third section (vv. 10–11) reverses the image of the uprooting of the braggart champion of evil by likening the psalmist to a growing olive tree in the house of God. The braggart is uprooted, the psalmist is deep-rooted; the braggart trusts in his own strength, the psalmist in the name of the Lord. The olive is a slow-growing tree, the very symbol of stability. It may take 30 years to reach its full fruiting capacity but will then continue to bear fruit for most of a millennium if it is tended with loving care, the sort of care an olive tree will receive in the house of God. Today many olive trees stand as a reminder on the Temple Mount, the area where the temple once stood. To harm a neighbour's olive tree is considered a heinous crime. The rape of olive orchards by governmental shifting of borders (for example, around Bethlehem) rankles more deeply with the Palestinians than almost any other hurt.

So, in Jeremiah 11:16, Israel is named by the Lord 'Green olive-tree covered in fine fruit'. In Romans 11, Paul again uses this figure in his consideration of the agonising enigma that Israel, so long prepared, has failed to respond to its Messiah. The Jews are the dead branches, cut off to make room for the ingrafting of the shoots of the wild olive, the Gentiles. But by some horticultural miracle ('How rich and deep are the wisdom and the knowledge of God! We cannot reach to the root of his decisions': Romans 11:33), the discarded branches will be grafted in again in the fullness of time.

Psalm 52[53]: The fool has said in his heart

In this psalm, the title is verse 1.

This psalm is an almost exact repeat of Psalm 13[14]. It uses the common noun 'God' as the name for the deity, whereas the earlier psalm uses the name YHWH, which is too intimate and too awesome to be pronounced. Apart from this, there are only slight variations in the description of the fate of the wicked in verse 6.

Psalm 53[54]: O God, save me by your name

In this psalm, the title is verses 1–2.

This last of the three successive little psalms about opposition falls neatly into two halves: the problem and the solution. The solution unfolds in just the same steps as the problem folded up:

Verse 3: Your name
 Verse 5a: The proud
  Verse 5b: My life
   Verse 5c: They have no regard for God
   Verse 6a: I have God for my help
  Verse 6b: My life
 Verse 7: My foes
Verses 8–9: Your name

How can a name, even the name of God, save? In biblical thought, the giving of a name is a serious matter. Adam completes the creation of the animals by giving them names, thus turning a formless hulk into something that can be grasped and recognised – a lion or mosquito or whatever (Genesis 2:19). When the mysterious stranger, having wrestled with Jacob, gives him the new name of 'Israel', he converts him from being a trickster who has cheated his father, brother and uncle into being a respectable patriarch, the 'Man Seeing God' (Ish-Ra-El: Genesis 32:29). Jesus gives the leader of his disciples the new name of 'Rock', that he may be the foundation of his Church (Matthew 16:18). Most significant of all, at the burning bush, Moses is given the special, unpronounceable name of God, but only later is given its meaning as 'a God of tenderness and mercy' (Exodus 34:6). In one psalm after another, God's name is something that provides shelter and security.

In the New Testament, more particularly in Acts, the name of Jesus, which means 'Saviour', takes on the same significance. Christians are defined as those who call on the name of Jesus as a security and protection, almost as a sort of talisman. Christians are baptised in the name – that is, in the power – of Jesus. They are also sometimes said to be baptised *into* the name of Jesus – that is, into the company of Jesus – thereby taking on a solidarity and participation with Jesus. Christians are also called those over whom the name of Jesus has been pronounced in blessing. In modern spirituality, perhaps especially in the eastern churches, this emphasis issues in the Jesus Prayer: 'Lord Jesus Christ, Son of God, have mercy on me.'

Psalm 54[55]: Give ear, O God, to my prayer

In this psalm, the title is verse 1.

This psalm is so varied that it is difficult to characterise. Clearly it is a psalm of lament, laying before the Lord the trouble that the psalmist is undergoing, but is the trouble a personal or a public difficulty? At times it seems personal ('my heart is stricken'); at times the danger seems public ('I see violence and strife in the city'). At times the enemies seem many ('those who fight me are many'); at times the central tragedy seems to be betrayal by a particular friend ('my friend whom I knew so well'). Perhaps the best solution is the suggestion that the poem has grown and expanded as it was used on several occasions, just as the writings of the prophets – perhaps especially the book of Isaiah – were used and reused, with slight adjustments to different contemporary situations. This would be typical of the development of oral tradition.

I am especially moved by two aspects. The first is the longing for the peace of the desert in verses 6–8. Israel always looked back with longing to the peace of the desert, the idyll of simple fidelity to the Lord during the wanderings of the exodus, the honeymoon period. The starkness of the deserts to the east and south of Jerusalem, the Judean desert and the Negeb, has an enduring attraction for the people with its nomadic past. These are gently rolling hills of buff-coloured rock, devoid of all but an occasional wisp of grass, where even the wild camels find little to crop. ('What does the camel find to eat?' I asked, on a visit there. 'The camel, he eat the ground,' replied the diminutive goatherd.) The stillness has a daunting majesty that both scares and elevates the soul. One can appreciate why Jesus went out into the desert after his baptism: he was with the wild beasts, and the angels ministered to him. One can appreciate, too, why the psalmist longed to escape his enemies and take refuge in the silent solitude of the desert.

The other moving aspect is the treachery of the trusted friend in verses 13–15 and 21–22, which the psalmist finds so hard to bear. The Christian cannot but be reminded of Judas. Jesus trusted him to the extent of making him the cashier of the group of disciples. Or was the triple denial by Peter, the 'Rock', in his hour of need, a more devastating betrayal? And what of my own betrayals?

Psalm 55[56]: In God I trust, I shall not fear

In this psalm, the title is verse 1.

The shape of this poem of fear and trust is straightforward. It has two parts (vv. 2–8 and 9–14), each anchored in the central refrain of invincible confidence in God's power to solve the problem (vv. 5, 11–12). Each half also ends with a firm statement of confidence (vv. 8, 13–14). Perhaps the most striking feature of the psalm is the repeated combination of fear and trust. The one never appears without the other, but the two are always together, balancing one another.

The psalm raises in sharp form the question, 'Who are these enemies?' There is mention of assailants and ambush, of rescue from death and of the foes turning back. These elements suggest real armed attack. But there is mention also of pride and verbal distortion by the enemies – a non-violent, verbal attack. Allied to this is the question, 'Who is represented as praying?' Commentators often place this and other such psalms in the mouth of a king, beleaguered by the armies of national enemies. This would place the psalms at the time of the Davidic monarchy, when kings engaged in both petty and major wars. Are we to believe that they took time off to compose such prayers, or that such prayers were ready to hand for them in the temple? While it seems most probable that the collection of psalms stems from the temple, we have no idea how it was formed or housed. In any case, the weight of scholarly opinion is that the majority of the psalms were composed during the Second Temple period, after the restoration from exile in Babylon, when kings (if they existed) played a much less prominent role.

In the course of the psalms, enemies are presented in a variety of guises, as packs of dogs roaming about the city, fierce bulls of Bashan, the horns of wild oxen, floods of water reaching high levels, nets or traps laid in the path, enemies patrolling the city walls night and day. If taken literally, these images would suggest an endemically violent, brutal and unstable society – an impression not borne out by the rest of biblical literature. It is better to understand these threats as vivid metaphors: 'their teeth are spears and arrows, their tongue a sharpened sword' (Psalm 56[57]:5). In prayer we know our own fallibility and proneness to be lured or scared from the right path. This psalm's combination of fear and trust is no bad image for the tightrope we walk.

Psalm 56[57]: Be exalted, O God, above the heavens!

In this psalm, the title is verse 1.

This psalm betrays the same context as the previous psalm in the collection, a balance between hostile threats and confidence in God. It falls into two halves, each concluding with the refrain, 'Be exalted above the heavens, O God; above all the earth is your glory' (vv. 6, 12). This gives the clue to a difference in this psalm compared with the previous one: it includes a cosmic dimension, involving not only the heavens but also the nations on earth. Correspondingly, it is no longer on the knife-edge, poised between fear on the one side and trust on the other, but is full of confidence and praise.

What are we to do with 'the heavens' in an age when a three-decker universe is out of fashion? It is no longer useful to conceive of God 'up there' in deist isolation. We concentrate much more on divine interpenetration of all things, the divine presence conserving creation from moment to moment. The idea of the heavens can, however, still contribute to this conception. 'Your love reaches to the heavens and your truth to the skies' (v. 11; see also v. 4) suggests the spread of these two divine influences, two divine ways of communicating with us – love and truth – right from us into the limitless, expanding universe. They fill the intervening space, and even the cyberspace as well!

This impression is confirmed by the final concentration in each half of the psalm on the divine glory. That wonderful concept of divine glory, both thrilling and awesome, reverses the movement, spreading not from earth as far as heaven but from heaven to earth, again filling the intervening space. So in the shadow of his wings I am wrapped not only in love and truth but also in the divine glory.

Another aspect of the cosmic dimension is the inclusion of the nations in the praise of God (v. 10). The Babylonian exile alerted Israel to other nations, who worshipped other gods, and to the question of how these nations were to be saved, since Israel saw more and more strongly that there was only one true God. The answer was that they were to be saved by Israel's God, and were to come to Jerusalem to draw salvation from there. So Israel becomes the focus for universal salvation. The nations, too, will draw waters from the wells of salvation, and will come bringing gifts to Israel's God. In the preparation for the gospel message to all nations, this becomes ever clearer, until in Zechariah 14 we have the great scene of the judgment day for all nations on the Mount of Olives: 'When that Day comes, the Lord will be the one and only and his name the one name' (v. 14).

Psalm 57[58]: Do you truly speak justice?

In this psalm, the title is verse 1.

This is one of the very few psalms not generally used in the public liturgy. It is used neither in the Roman Breviary nor in the Common Lectionary. This is less because the text is highly corrupt, and is reconstructed in very different ways, than because it is lusciously vindictive.

Judges hold the divine power of judgment, and all public judgment should echo and prolong the judgment of God. The Law consistently teaches that if Israel is to be the people of God, it must treat the widow, the immigrant and the orphan as God himself treated the Israelites when they were immigrants in Egypt – but this did not always happen. In a less strictly controlled system of justice, the rich had plenty of opportunity to make themselves richer through the administration of justice, instead of righting injustice. From the earliest prophets onwards, Amos, Hosea and the other messengers of God's word constantly reproached the rich for misusing their power as judges and administrators, falsifying weights and measures to their own advantage, accepting bribes and so on. This psalm joins its voice to those of the prophets. The problem, indeed, persists. There are plenty of situations in the modern world, even in Christian countries, where injustice is officially done and the downtrodden have no hope of redress.

However, in the psalm, wicked judges are vituperated in terms that go far beyond modern political correctness, almost as though the author is delighting in his colourful vituperation for its own sake. Liturgists no doubt felt that the terms were too violent to be edifying or prayerful. The same is true of the splendidly constructed and detailed curse in the most famous of all Cursing Psalms, Psalm 108(109). These unjust judges are first described in the most colourful terms as venomous snakes refusing to obey the snake charmer: evidently the African horned viper was considered to be deaf because it has no visible hearing apparatus. Then their retribution is described in terms of extreme and pitiless violence: teeth broken in the mouth, snails dissolving into slime. The psalm ends on a note of satisfaction, with the righteous bathing their feet in the blood of the wicked.

Psalm 58[59]: Rescue me, God, from my foes

In this psalm, the title is verse 1.

The violence of this psalm is its most striking feature – both the threatening violence of the psalmist's enemies and the violence that he prays his God to visit upon them. We do not know the context of this energetic and colourful prayer, but hints allow us at least to imagine a context for it. The basis of it is spatial: at the centre is the psalmist, clinging to his divine Protector, his Strength, his God in whom he trusts. He makes an urgent plea for protection, coupled with insistent protestations of innocence (vv. 4-5). In the background is an encircling miasma of predatory beasts, twice described as howling like dogs as they roam about the city each evening (vv. 7, 15-16). The psalmist veers between praying for their violent and merciless annihilation and mitigating his plea to a request that they be allowed to remain as a reminder of God's protective power while God merely laughs at them.

The context may be imagined (but with no certainty) as the biblical institution of sanctuary. Joshua 20 makes provision for six cities of refuge, scattered throughout the promised land, to which an unintentional killer may flee for sanctuary. In the rough system of justice practised in those days (and still among the local Arab tribes), the family of the killed man was obliged to exact vengeance from the killer, regardless of blame. The killer could take refuge in these cities until a trial before the community could be sorted out. However, this privilege may have been more notional than real. The only recorded instance of its successful use seems to have been Adonijah's flight to the altar in fear of Solomon's anger (1 Kings 1:50). Soon afterwards, the veteran general Joab, a supporter of Adonijah, attempted to use the same privilege. But he was too formidable an opponent to be allowed to live, and Solomon audaciously had him cut down at the altar itself (1 Kings 2:28–34).

In medieval times, churches provided sanctuary from arrest under some conditions, and even in modern society the same appeal to divine protection has occasionally been successful, principally in cases of illegal immigration. This is a moving case of residual respect for the protective power of the divinity (however this divinity may be envisaged) as at least a guarantee of fair play in a professedly post-Christian world. How much more assured in the world of the psalmist was the protection of the Lord against these raiders of the night!

Psalm 59[60]: With God we shall do bravely

In this psalm, the title is verses 1–2.

The attitude expressed by this psalm could be described as 'confidence in defeat'. The first section (vv. 3–7) characterises a military defeat in the apocalyptic terms of an earthquake. The use of such language in Hebrew poetry is frequent. Nor is it absent from sports journalism in English! Drinking a cup is a frequent image of swallowing some bitterness – 'taking the medicine' (Isaiah 51:17, 20–21) – used of course also by Jesus to the sons of Zebedee (Mark 10:38–39) and in his own time of agony in Gethsemane (Mark 14:36).

Immediately after this unpromising start, the psalmist launches paradoxically into confident claims for various parts of the territory distributed by Joshua. First, two cities of northern Israel, Shechem and Succoth, are claimed for God. This suggests that the psalm was written in Judah after the return from exile, when the northern kingdom was in the hands of foreigners, the Samaritans. Then larger northern territories, Gilead and Manasseh, are claimed. Finally Ephraim (just north of Jerusalem) and Judah itself are claimed. The status of these two areas is different, for Ephraim has the dignity of being the helmet of the Lord, while Judah has the highest prize, as God's own sceptre. In contrast to the others, both these mentions are very complimentary.

Next the psalmist turns to the traditional enemies of Israel. The Philistines had been the main enemies in the early period, increasingly encroaching on Israel until defeated and repulsed by King David. Then they virtually ceased to exist, although they gave their name to the country of 'Palestine'. After this the psalmist turns to two large territories east of the Jordan which had constantly been thorns in Israel's flesh. Moab had taken part in the plundering of Jerusalem at the time of the exile; it is to be no more than God's washbowl. The worst of the traditional enemies was Edom, against whom there had been constant wars; God's casting his shoe on Edom must be an insulting gesture of appropriation, though there is no real biblical parallel for this figure.

After these brave claims, the psalmist seems to lose confidence again, asking whether God has, after all, rejected Israel and begging for God's help against the enemy. The psalm need not necessarily be regarded as belligerent, for there is no talk of violent destruction of the enemy. It should rather been seen as a statement of God's sovereignty over the whole earth and special patronage of Israel.

Psalm 60[61]: My refuge and my mighty tower

In this psalm, the title is verse 1.

This is a simple little psalm of confidence. It falls into two halves, articulated round the verb 'hear'. This is more obvious in the Hebrew. The first four verses begin with the cry 'Hear, O God!' and make a confident request that God will hear the psalmist's prayer. The second four (vv. 6–9) begin 'You, O God, have heard' and spell out the blessings of which the psalmist is confident. So the first half constitutes the request, the second the fulfilment of that request.

This makes more sense than other emphases. Some commentators stress the cry 'from the end of the earth' (v. 3) and attribute the psalm to a singer in the first deportation to Babylon, while a king was still on the throne of Jerusalem. Others are drawn by the mention of the king (v. 7) to make the king the singer of the psalm – speaking of himself in the third person.

Two details are particularly attractive. The first is 'the rock too high for me to reach' (v. 3). This plays on a characteristic feature of the Holy Land. Among its amazing variety of landscapes is a series of high and rocky peaks, cut off by unassailable cliffs and crowned by castles of many ages – prehistoric, Canaanite, Herodian (King Herod was a great builder), Crusader. Well might the psalmist pray to be set on one of these impregnable peaks as a tower against the foe! Before the invention of gunpowder, they were a refuge that no enemy could penetrate.

The second detail is the messianic prayer for the king (v. 8). There is a sure allusion here to the promises given by the prophet Nathan to David (2 Samuel 7): his heirs will be enthroned forever before God. Their throne will be founded on and guaranteed by the family love or paternal love (*hesed*) of God, and by God's unfailing fidelity to his promises. These promises were never fulfilled by the line of kings in the Old Testament. Instead, the prophets continued to look forward to their fulfilment in the Messiah whom God would send to bring the kingship of God to completion at the end of time. We see them to be fulfilled in Jesus the Christ. As the prologue to the gospel of John concludes, 'The Law came through Moses, grace and truth through Jesus Christ' (John 1:17). 'Grace and truth' are the family love and the fulfilment promised in this psalm.

Psalm 61[62]: In God alone is my soul at rest

In this psalm, the title is verse 1.

We can divide this psalm into three sections. The first two begin with a sort of refrain (vv. 2–3, 6–7), identical in the two cases but for one crucial exception: the first refrain sees God as the source of salvation, the second as the source of hope. These two key words provide enough to meditate on for the course of the whole psalm. Both are the basis of any stability.

'Salvation' often carries an allusion to the events of the past, to the exodus from Egypt, when God delivered his people from the misery of slavery and the perils of pursuit, and again to the deliverance from captivity in Babylon. For the Christian, though, the sense is further enriched because the name 'Jesus' is the same word in Hebrew. For us, the concept of salvation is captured by and focused on Jesus. He is the Saviour, and in him God the Saviour brings his ancient work of salvation to completion. For a Christian, the idea of 'hope', the second key word of the refrains, is also no vague concept. It is the confidence in things to come. The letter to the Hebrews is the most burning scriptural expression of hope, with its deep conviction of pilgrimage; it sees the people of God journeying restlessly to the place of rest promised to them but never reached in the Old Testament (Hebrews 4:1–13).

After each of these two initial refrains comes a comment. The first (vv. 4–5) is negative, describing the attack of enemies on God's faithful one as though he were (splendid images!) 'a tottering wall or a tumbling fence'. The second (vv. 8–9) is positive, a joyful confirmation of the refrain, full of strong and positive words: 'salvation', 'glory', 'strength' and 'refuge'.

The third section of the psalm is quite different and is the first occurrence for some time of a Wisdom passage. The Wisdom literature is always instructional, reflecting on life and humanity, on human capacities and follies. In the days towards the end of the Old Testament period, when there seemed to be no more prophets to guide God's people, great collections of Wisdom sayings and proverbs were made, which found their way into the collection of writings we now call the Bible. The last section of this psalm (vv. 10–13) is just such a little collection of reflections. It has a lovely build-up. Verse 10 starts with the inanity of human powers. The key word is *hebel*, which features so prominently in the book of Ecclesiastes: 'vanity of vanities', a mere breath – passing, swiftly dissipated and utterly forgotten. Verse 11 paints the consequences: no human wealth or plunder can satisfy. Then verse 12 comes crashing in with the opposite, the power of God and his love, which really are effective.

Psalm 62[63]: My soul thirsts for God

In this psalm, the title is verse 1.

This yearning psalm is the climax of a set of three. Psalm 60[61] was a prayer of quiet confidence that God would hear the psalmist's requests. Psalm 61[62] was suffused with the themes of hope and salvation. Now we have a picture of the psalmist secure in attachment to the Lord. The tenses of the Hebrew verbs used here imply a continuous state of seeking, thirsting, pining. This is no temporary state but the condition that is the foundation of the psalmist's being – confident attachment to God – so that 'thirsts' and 'pines' better yield the sense of the original than 'is thirsting' and 'is pining'.

I once got lost in the Judean desert, crossing it from Jerusalem to the Dead Sea with two strapping young friends. It was my own silly fault in map-reading. We ran out of water and really knew what 'a dry, weary land without water' (v. 2) meant. Just as we were stumbling to a standstill, the Lord provided a Jeep out of nowhere. It is at such times that one realises the blessing of water, and even perceives the 'strength and glory' of God. Although the psalmist has come before God 'in the holy place', the place is not important, for he nestles with God at the banquet and also through the night watches, permanently enjoying the presence of God.

For Christians, the banquet immediately suggests the messianic banquet at the end of time, the image so often used by Jesus in his parables of the last times and his sayings about the bridegroom, when God invites (indeed, presses) even sinners to join in the feast. Is there even a suggestion of life after death in 'your love is better than life' (v. 4)? We find the same thought in Paul: 'Life to me, of course, is Christ, but then death would be a positive gain' (Philippians 1:21). At the time of the psalmist, Israel had not yet been granted the full revelation of life after death, but is this already a hint, a suggestion that the love of God is so intense that it survives even physical death? Job had already proclaimed in his suffering, 'I know that after my awakening he will set me close to him' (Job 19:26). God will not let go of all those whom he loves, for 'he is God not of the dead but of the living' (Mark 12:27). That makes a fitting climax to these three psalms of confident praise.

Psalm 63[64]: Hear, O God, the voice of my complaint

In this psalm, the title is verse 1.

Some of the psalms present a strange mixture of emotions, including emotions we should not like to admit to sharing. So this psalm, after a brief initial plea to God for protection, goes on to dwell at length on the malice of the psalmist's opponents before gleefully reflecting on the revenge that God will inflict on them – to the complacent satisfaction of the psalmist. How can this be the material of Christian prayer? How can I make this prayer my own?

Are you sure that you never experience a twinge of satisfaction at the discomfiture of someone who has upset or hurt you? The psalmist makes no bones about it. Yet the psalmist is writing before Jesus' teaching on total forgiveness. In the Old Testament, proportionate revenge between opponents ('an eye for an eye, a tooth for a tooth') was still acceptable. The Israelites do not seem to have realised that human beings, made in the image of God, are called to imitate God's total forgiveness. This new stress by Jesus, especially in the Sermon on the Mount, gives us cause for joy, and also for self-examination. Heaven forbid that I should take revenge, but is there still a trace of pleasure in me when someone else does the job for me, when my opponent's secret malice is laid bare, when 'their own tongue has brought them to ruin'?

What about the final verse? Can I apply that to myself with an easy conscience? It contains two descriptions to which I certainly aspire. 'The righteous' is someone who puts all possible focus on obedience to and imitation of God as God's nature is revealed in the divine Law. Similarly, 'upright of heart' is a lovely description: in the Hebrew ('straight of heart') it suggests total straightforwardness and honesty, a smiling openness that always rejoices the heart. This psalm helps us remember that God's process of revelation is a continuous movement: there are elements in the Old Testament that Jesus' revelation will surpass. In the same way, our faulty individual spirituality is in constant need of progress and purification.

Psalm 64[65]: Praise is due to you in Zion, O God

In this psalm, the title is verse 1.

This psalm is, of course, a temple prayer. The worshippers are gathered in the temple of Jerusalem. They begin with a reflection on human inadequacy before God: we cannot stand before God unless God himself wipes away all our weight of transgressions. Just as every Christian Eucharist and Evensong begins with an acknowledgment of our failures and inadequacy, so this prayer puts the record straight right from the beginning by acknowledging our need to be called, chosen and forgiven if we are to face God in prayer.

Attention can then turn to the wonderful way in which God renews the world, particularly by the cycle of the crops. The praise begins, however, with the framework, the stability of the world (vv. 7–10). God's beneficent influence extends to the far distant isles, to the lands of sunrise and sunset, up to the heights of the mountains and down to the depths of the seas. The 'roaring of the seas' is almost viewed as their homage to God, their expression of joy in the Lord. Often in the Psalms (see 88[89]:9; 106[107]:29), control of the seas is viewed as the supreme instance of divine power. There is no other such mighty force of nature as the sea. Not even modern technology has made significant steps to harness or control it. The winds can be harvested and channelled, but the sea works its will despite all human ingenuity. The Christian may see here a hint giving its full meaning to the miracle of the calming of the storm by Jesus, which strikes such uncomprehending awe into his disciples (Mark 4:39–41). Imbued with the tradition that the mighty waters are under the direct control of God, the disciples are astonished that any mere man can exert this power: 'What manner of man is this?'

The chief focus of the psalm comes in God's beneficent gift of water to drench the parched earth and bring out its fruitfulness. The Psalms were written in a land where the barefoot children dance ecstatically for joy at the arrival of the first rains, gleefully kicking sheets of water at one another. It will mean a generous harvest and food for all. The dried-up streams will flow again, the underground aquifers be replenished and water be available at the dip of a bucket. Within days, the browned-off hills will show a delicate sheen of green, and shy wildflowers appear in the desert. 'They shout for joy, yes they sing!'

Psalm 65[66]: Cry out with joy to God, all the earth

The structure and direction of this psalm are not easy to grasp. Is it indeed a single prayer, or two joined together? There is a sharp disjunction between the two parts, but also a degree of balance, which may show that the two were envisaged together.

The first part (vv. 1–12) consists of three summonses: 'Cry out with joy to God' (v. 1), 'Come and see the works of God' (v. 5) and 'O peoples, bless our God' (v. 8). The reason for praising God seems to be God's glorious name, as seen in his great deeds. There is an allusion to the events of the exodus when the people crossed the sea and the river dryshod (v. 6), and then to a more testing time in which God 'laid a heavy burden on our backs' (v. 11). The latter may be a reference to the Babylonian exile, which is often seen as a time of purification, as in verse 10; it ends peacefully with 'but then you brought us relief', which may signify the return from exile. The whole is a trusting prayer, praising God for the continuing care of Israel throughout its history.

The second part (vv. 13–20) has a different tone, expressed chiefly in a dozen uses of the first person singular ('I', 'my'). It is no longer a community prayer but seems to be the prayer of an individual, perhaps a leader, who has the resources to offer quantities of bullocks, goats and sacrificial rams. It is not a summons to prayer and praise but, rather, a declaration of offering and of satisfaction that his prayer has been heard and accepted (vv. 19–20). The burnt offerings and the vow-sacrifice that the psalmist brings are primarily expressions of gratitude and celebration; the burnt offering is wholly consumed by fire, but the vow-sacrifice normally includes a celebratory meal. Thus the theme is gratitude for God's response to the psalmist's prayer for deliverance from distress, a gratitude that he wants to share with 'all who fear God'. No doubt they would share the celebratory meal, too!

The two halves are linked together by two features. The first is 'Come and see' in the first half, balanced by 'Come and hear' in the second (vv. 5 and 16 respectively). The second linking feature is the inversion in the two halves:

Verses 1–9: summons to prayer
    Verses 10–12: direct prayer to God
    Verses 13–15: direct prayer to God
Verses 16–20: summons to share

Psalm 66[67]: Let all the peoples praise you

In this psalm, the title is verse 1.

This cheerful short psalm falls clearly into three stanzas, separated by the two refrains. It can, but need not, be viewed as a sort of double sandwich (technically, 'chiastic in form'), the first and third stanzas corresponding to each other, with the principal stress on the central stanza. In any case, each stanza has its special contribution to make. (There is no textual warrant for repeating the refrain a third time, though some modern editions print it a third time.)

The first stanza, which sets the joyful tone of the psalm, grows out of the triple formula for blessing entrusted to Aaron and his priestly descendants: 'May the Lord bless you and keep you. May the Lord let his face shine on you and be gracious to you. May the Lord show you his face and bring you peace' (Numbers 6:24).

The Aaronic blessing, however, includes no mention of blessing on the other nations. It was only at the time of the Babylonian exile, confronted with Babylonian idolatry, that Israel began to be conscious of its mission to the world. God's choice was not a private matter between the Lord and Israel. Rather, during the Babylonian exile Israel began to see that Israel's task was to bring the power and salvation of God to the other nations. The nations were to come to Jerusalem to draw water from the wells of salvation. This theme becomes ever more important in the later prophets, from the later parts of Isaiah onwards. This aspect must have been at least in the background of the apostle Paul's thinking, so that he was ready for the revelation that his mission was to the Gentiles, to include them in the salvation promised to Abraham. This theme song is echoed in the refrain, with its mention of all the nations 'praising you, O God'.

The third stanza is a thanksgiving for the harvest: 'the earth has yielded its fruit'. This gives a context for the blessing of God and the cheerfulness of the psalm. In an agricultural society, a good or bad harvest sets the tone for the whole year, and in this case the rejoicing for the good harvest as an indication of God's blessing is extended to the whole earth.

The keynote second stanza is a celebration of God's rule over the whole world. If God rules the world with justice, then there is stability and fairness and all is well with the universe. From this fan out all other benefits and causes for praise. St Benedict prescribed that this celebration should always begin the monastic morning prayer of praise.

Psalm 67[68]: Let God arise; let his foes be scattered

In this psalm, the title is verse 1.

This great processional hymn celebrates God going up to his sanctuary in Jerusalem. Although we know nothing from the rest of the Bible about a procession to the temple, we must assume that at some stage in the year such a procession took place, commemorating the arrival of God in his holy place. It may well have a basis in the procession described in 2 Samuel 6, when David brought the ark of the covenant up to his newly conquered capital, making Jerusalem not only his own capital but God's capital too. It is difficult to believe that this whole scenario of a procession is purely imaginary. 'Let God arise,' begins the celebration, as the bearers lift up the ark.

The hymn is rich in imagery, some primitive or even barbaric. God is represented as a God of thunder and lightning, a God of desert storm, riding on the clouds, as did Baal, the storm-god of the Canaanites. There are traces of some rivalry between the great mountains of the north, Hermon, Zalmon and Bashan, and the smaller but centrally placed hill of Zion in Jerusalem. Equally prominent is the bloodthirsty imagery of an exultant conquest hymn, describing feet bathed in blood and dogs taking their share, as well as women arraying themselves in the spoils of victory. Such brutal and even braggart imagery is well known from the great victory inscriptions of the surrounding nations that survive on stone pillars. To us, it seems to clash with the gentler appreciation of God as father of orphans and defender of widows, but the two aspects are combined in Israel's expression of an all-powerful and all-loving God who is served by the strong and cares for the weak.

Striking, also, are the glimpses of the physical composition of the procession: singers at the front, instrumentalists at the back and more delicate drum majorettes in between. For some reason, the procession is headed by the smallest of all the tribes, Benjamin, from just north of Jerusalem, followed by the massed leaders of Judah, the greatest of the southern tribes. Of other tribes, only Zebulun and Naphtali, both from the far north in what is now Galilee, gain a mention. The homage of other nations is represented by merchants from Egypt and Ethiopia. The psalm is shot through with an awareness that the powerful God of the whole earth is being welcomed to the single sanctuary where his presence and his care will be focused on Israel.

Psalm 68[69]: Save me, O God, for the waters have risen

In this psalm, the title is verse 1.

Lamentation is the keynote of this psalm. The psalmist alternates between pleas for help or deliverance and a description of the trouble he is in. The trouble is described in the dramatic imagery of sinking into mud and being overwhelmed by floods, but also more soberly in terms of personal opposition, false accusation, taunts, gossip and attempted poisoning. Although he is content to confess 'sinful folly' to the Lord (v. 6), the psalmist can also claim that he is undergoing the taunts for the sake of the Lord (v. 8). In any case, the opposition is clearly felt to be out of all proportion to what is deserved. Even acts of penance, like wearing sackcloth, are greeted only with derision. Then suddenly, at the end, after purging himself by a round of cursing on his enemies, the psalmist suddenly cheers up and devotes himself to praise of the Lord and prediction of national return to Zion from exile. This is enough to show that the psalm dates from the end of the exile. The oft-quoted parallel with the pathetic story of Jeremiah being dumped in the mud of an empty water-cistern is hardly relevant (see Jeremiah 38:6).

Perhaps more important to us than this doleful psalm itself is the frequency of allusion to it found in the New Testament. There, the psalmist is seen to be Jesus, especially in his role as the innocent sufferer. So, in John 2:17, the cleansing of the temple is seen to be a fulfilment of 'I burn with zeal for your house'. In John 15:25, the unjustified opposition to Jesus is seen to fulfil 'those that hate without cause'. At the scene of the crucifixion, the proffered drink (Mark 15:36) is seen as a fulfilment of 'they gave me vinegar to drink', and Matthew 27:34 adds an allusion to 'for food they gave me poison'. In Acts 1:20, the curse on the taunting enemies of the sufferer is seen as fulfilled in the death of Judas: 'let their camp be left desolate'.

It was important to show that the events culminating in Jesus' humiliating death on the cross were the fulfilment of God's plan revealed in scripture. In accordance with the principles of scriptural exegesis current in New Testament times (and seen most clearly in the Dead Sea Scrolls), this was done by detailed and atomistic allusion. In modern times we would see it more as a fulfilment of the whole thrust of scripture and of the whole history of Israel.

Psalm 69[70] O God, come to my assistance!

In this psalm, the title is verse 1.

This psalm is almost identical to Psalm 39(40):14–18. The chief difference is that in the Hebrew of Psalm 39(40) the divine name YHWH is used, as in all the psalms of that collection. It is difficult to say which of the two is the original version.

Psalm 70[71]: In you, O Lord, I take refuge

There is something delightfully stable and traditional about this psalm. The language is familiar, and often the psalmist seems to be adopting phrases or whole lines from other psalms (for example, verses 1–3 are almost identical to 30[31]:1–3; verse 13 virtually repeats Psalm 39[40]:14). The psalmist begins by looking back to the way the Lord has helped him from his youth, from his mother's womb (v. 6), repeating the idea in verse 17; for old people, their clearest memories are often of childhood. Twice he mentions that he has grown old (vv. 9, 18). The stability is increased by the frequent use of 'always' and 'all the day long'. In general, we have the impression that this psalmist is an older person. He is not looking for excitement or novelty, but is rejoicing in the way God has cared for him up till now (he mentions that his life has not been without difficulties) and praying that this care may continue.

The basic concepts of the psalm, too, to which the psalmist returns again and again, are the reliable and traditional concepts of God's fidelity to his promises, his righteousness, and his salvation or saving power. God's justice, or righteousness, is not an exacting or avenging power but a saving justice: that is, it shows the absolute dependability for us of the promises given to Abraham and repeated to all the patriarchs. This is the concept that Paul will pick up, making it the basis of his letter to the Romans – God's saving justice revealed in Christ and especially in his passion, death and resurrection.

The psalmist speaks in the same vein of God's salvation and redemption: in the Old Testament, God acts as Saviour and Redeemer primarily through his deliverance of Israel from slavery in Egypt and from other hostile forces. The title is ready for its transference to Jesus, our Saviour and Redeemer, which makes it, by allusion, a divine title.

God is a rock and a stronghold against the oppressor. Another special concept is 'the Holy One of Israel', a favourite character-isation of God throughout the book of Isaiah, given light in the wonderful vision of the holiness of God in Isaiah 6. All these are loving, affectionate ways in which the psalmist praises God.

Psalm 71[72]: O God, give your judgment to the king

We have not had a messianic psalm since the royal wedding song of Psalm 44[45]. The seams between the books of Psalms are marked by messianic psalms, and this one concludes the second book. The final two verses of the psalm form a doxology for the whole book, rather than belonging specifically to this psalm. Similar doxologies occur at 40[41]:13; 88[89]:53; 105[106]:48 and, finally, the whole of Psalms 148—150.

The attraction of this particular royal psalm is its peacefulness. There is no suggestion of military domination or bloody victory, only of responsible rule and care for the poor and needy. This is all the more remarkable given that, in those days, power was conceived overwhelmingly in terms of weaponry and military prowess. Such an ideal of monarchy as care for the subject peoples did indeed exist in the ancient Near East, but hardly ever had this prominence. Again and again, we find a recurring stress on attention to the weak, the needy, the poor and oppressed. In this psalm the only fawning of enemies is provided by the creatures in verse 9 (*zi'im* in Hebrew), translated variously as 'desert-dwellers' or 'wild cats', scary creatures who take up residence in and haunt eerie ruins (Isaiah 13:21; Jeremiah 50:39). Even they will be tamed!

This is the kingdom that Jesus will declare and newly inaugurate by his works of healing and forgiveness, his welcome offered to lepers and outcasts and his divine generosity to all who will listen. This is the translation into leadership terms of God's promises to Abraham that he would care for his descendants always. This may be why the title of this psalm is uniquely given as 'For Solomon', in accordance with Solomon's prayer at the beginning of his reign, for wisdom rather than wealth or the lives of his enemies (1 Kings 3). The tribute from the kings of Sheba, Tarshish and the islands, and the gold of Sheba, may also be linked to the famous visit of the Queen of Sheba to Solomon (1 Kings 10). It also chimes in with the visit to Jerusalem of the far-flung monarchs of Tarshish, Sheba and elsewhere to pay honour to and rejoice in the light of Jerusalem, in Isaiah 60.

As a celebration of any earthly monarch, the language is flattering and grossly exaggerated; no human king will rule 'from sea to sea' (v. 8), and no human rule will 'endure like the sun and the moon from age to age (v. 5). Beneath the hyperbole, however, shimmers the worldwide beneficent rule of God's own Messiah.

Book 3

Psalm 72[73]: To be near God is my happiness

It won't do – or will it? The psalmist is getting to grips with one of the problems of evil: how is it that the wicked prosper and sleekly preen themselves on prospering? But does he lose the courage of his convictions in the end?

The problem is at its most acute in the book of Job. We are clearly told there that Job's sufferings are undeserved, but no solution is given beyond the awe-inspiring speeches of God in the final chapters. They tell us that we cannot see the solution, and with our puny human minds we have no right to subject the limitless power and limitless wisdom of God to interrogation.

In this psalm, it is put differently. After a brief sentence of acclaim to God, the psalmist devotes verses 2–14 to a witty panegyric of how the wicked prosper and win the flattery of all around them (or perhaps below them). Then he suddenly checks himself and chides himself for these thoughts, rejecting them as unworthy of Israel (v. 15). So in verses 18–20 he puts the opposite point of view, that the prosperity of the wicked is short-lived. What, then, is the solution?

A conventional Christian approach is to invoke a reward in the next life, 'when everything is made new again and the Son of Man is seated on his throne' (Matthew 19:28) or 'you will eat and drink at my table' (Luke 18:30). Our psalmist, however, shows no sign of any awareness of life after death. It is simply not a factor in the discussion, as it is not yet part of Israel's thinking. 'What else have I in heaven but you?' (v. 25) does not imply an afterlife residence in heaven. The Hebrew would be more accurately translated, 'What is there to me in the heavens?' The psalmist's solution is nobler than that. It is simply to keep company with God: 'Apart from you I want nothing on earth.'

In Christian thinking also, to be face to face in the presence of God, bathed in the overflowing love of God, is the essence of the joy of heaven. The book of Revelation (22:5) tells us that God and the Lamb is (not 'are') the light and the temple in the new Jerusalem, and there is no need for any other. Centuries before, the psalmist already had the same instinct: 'To be near God is my happiness' (v. 28).

Psalm 73[74]: Why, O God, have you cast us off forever?

This is perhaps the saddest and most distressing of all the psalms. It leaves the sound of hatchet and pickaxe echoing in the head, evoking the brutal destruction of everything that Israel held dear and sacred, which left the blasphemous pagan standards reigning over the ruins. From this psalm, more than from any other writing, we get the impression of the shock and bewilderment wrought by the Babylonian destruction of the temple and city in 587BC. How can God, Israel's champion and all-powerful defender, who created and controls the world, have allowed it to happen? God has not even left them a prophet to explain the meaning of the events.

The structure of the lament is simple and obvious:

- Verses 1–11: the horrors of destruction
- Verses 12–17: puzzled astonishment that the God who controls creation (the monstrous sea-beasts, the mythical Leviathan himself, the very sources of water, the light, the sun and the seasons) should have allowed this to happen
- Verses 18–23: a plea, in the name of the covenant, for restoration

Well, then, how did it happen? The prophets Jeremiah and Ezekiel and the Deuteronomic writers, all theologians of Israel's troubled history, had no doubts. This terrible devastation, in which they lost everything they held dear – king, city, temple, worship rituals, priesthood, the land itself – was all brought on by Israel's persistent infidelity to the covenant. Warning after warning was neglected, until God had no alternative than to leave the brutal Babylonian war-machine to take its course. It seemed to be the end of everything, and yet, in Babylon, Israel re-formed, developing a more chastened, committed way of life and a more sensitive, open view of the nation's vocation from God. The tribal covenant would be transformed into a new covenant with every individual, making an individual and vibrant link between God and each of those who put their trust in him. Together, these transformations would prepare the Jews for the coming of the Lord's Messiah.

In Ezekiel 36:16–36, the prophet has his own way of putting this: Israel has profaned the name of God, making it look as though Yahweh could not even protect his own people, to whom he had bound himself by covenant, and so making him the laughing-stock of the nations. But he will pour clean water over them, remove the heart of stone from their bodies and give them a heart of flesh instead, putting his Spirit in them. Then he will clear his great name by leading them back to their own land to fulfil his purpose. This is what we mean each time we pray, 'Hallowed be thy name.'

Psalm 74[75]: The Lord holds a cup in his hand

In this psalm, the title is verse 1.

This psalm reasserts the Lord's strength and control against all human arrogance, and the Lord's retribution of the wicked. It may be, therefore, that it was placed after the devastating statement in the previous psalm of the desecration of the temple by blasphemous human brutality as a deliberate comment on that desecration. Taken by itself, however, the psalm is a simple statement of God's control of the world and retribution of wrongdoing, particularly arrogance.

The dramatic speaker changes in the course of the psalm, and it is not easy to decide who is speaking in each verse. However, the following distribution seems sensible.

- Verse 2 is a general statement of praise and affirmation of God.
- In verses 3-6, God speaks, asserting his control over creation and rebuking the proud who flaunt their own strength and independence. In particular, the statement uses the splendid imagery of God setting firm the pillars of the world. The Hebrews envisaged the earth as a flat plate, surmounted by the dome of heaven. The whole was surrounded by the limitless mass of waters, held back from crushing the world only by the power of God. It was pictured as resting on pillars set in the waters and held firm by God. (This only partly makes sense, for what was the point of the pillars unless they rested on something?)
- At verse 7 the psalmist takes over, echoing the idea that God alone assigns honour and power. This is stressed (v. 9) by the dread image of the cup of wrath, vividly portrayed by the prophets (Isaiah 51:17; Jeremiah 25:15-18) and the book of Revelation (14:10), which those who set themselves against God will be forced to drink to the dregs. The psalm ends with the quiet contentment of confidence in God.

The spirituality of this psalm is closely reminiscent of the tone of Luke's infancy narratives. These first two chapters of the gospel, especially the canticles in the mouths of Zechariah and Mary, are filled with confidence in God's power to bring down the mighty from their thrones and exalt the lowly. An attractive contrast is provided by the horn, symbol of strength. Here in verse 5 the wicked are told (literally) not to lift up their horn, since God humbles and exalts. By contrast, in the Benedictus, Zechariah rejoices that God has raised up a horn of salvation in the house of David his servant (Luke 1:69). The great scriptural scholar Origen (185-254) saw this as referring to Christ himself; others interpret it more widely as the whole thrust towards salvation in Christ.

Psalm 75[76]: God is renowned in Judah

In this psalm, the title is verse 1.

The occasion for the composition of this psalm can no longer be recovered, but it is clearly celebrating the majesty of the Lord in his sanctuary in Jerusalem. The opening verses suggest a stunning victory at Jerusalem itself – possibly as a reflection on Sennacherib's mighty Assyrian forces, which in 701BC ravaged all the other cities of Judah but mysteriously turned away from the gates of Jerusalem itself. Alternatively, 'horse and rider lay stunned' in verse 7 might suggest the discomfiture of Pharaoh's chariot drivers at the crossing of the Red Sea. I prefer to read both these particular references in a generalised sense, as expressions of the towering power of the Lord in Jerusalem. Divine victory, wherever it may be, sweeps all before it; there is simply no room for resistance.

This psalm is a particular case in which translations fall flat and fail to convey the awesomeness of the original. Everyday English words do not transmit the aura of which the Hebrew words, enriched by their sacred overtones in their biblical context, are redolent. For instance, the word *'adir*, translated in verse 5 as 'majestic', is used so frequently in the psalms alone of the daunting, unapproachable power of God (Psalms 8:1, 9; 92[93]:4), not to mention Exodus 15:11 and Isaiah 33:21, that the human response can only be awe and reverence. Several of the other expressions applied to God in this poem have the same inbuilt quality. 'The earth in terror was still' (v. 9) evokes the eerie silence that grips the countryside at a total eclipse of the sun, when birds and beasts fall silent with a preternatural silence, as though in dread and awe. In a world free from the perpetual roar of traffic and hum of electricity, the ear would be far more sensitive to a total silence.

In a totally different direction, 'the humble of the earth' (*'anawe*) is so frequently used of the Lord's special favourites, who have no strength of their own but rely entirely on the Lord, that it immediately evokes God's loving patronage. These are the poor and helpless, to whom the Lord comes in Luke 1—2 in the persons of Zechariah and Elizabeth, Mary herself and the nocturnal hireling shepherds. In both these cases, the Hebrew words, from their biblical associations, trigger a response that the English words do not. Translations can never be completely relied on!

Psalm 76[77]: Has the way of the Most High changed?

In this psalm, the title is verse 1.

This is a psalm whose sequence of thought is difficult to unravel. The latter part (vv. 12–21) is clear enough, referring in poetic and dramatic terms to the wonder of God's power in leading Israel across the Sea of Reeds, the primal miracle of the exodus from Egypt. The description recalls all the splendour of a tropical rainstorm with thunder and lightning and the whole of nature in turmoil. Israel loved to depict the mighty power of God in terms of the waters – a reminder that, by the Hebrew conception of creation, the universe is surrounded by water, no more than a bubble in the midst of the immense power of the water and its waves. If God were not permanently holding back the waters, they would rush in to envelop and crush the universe. In the dramatic description of these verses, the psalm focuses the struggle between God and the waters on the parting of the sea at the exodus. This historical reference is made clear by the names at beginning and end, 'the sons of Jacob and Joseph' (v. 16) and 'the hand of Moses and Aaron' (v. 21). The waters tremble and are moved with terror at the onslaught of God in his thunder and lightning, as he moves, majestically unseen, through the waves (v. 20).

But what of the earlier part of the psalm? Prayer no longer seems to be answered. I cry aloud, but to no avail. A shaft of doubt creeps in: has the powerful right hand of the Most High now changed? We have always been able to rely on the Lord, both in prayer (vv. 2–10) and in remembering the wonder of the crossing of the sea (vv. 12–21), but is the situation now different? The question is left unresolved at the end of the psalm, which seems to lack any conclusion after the recital of the people being guided through the sea like a flock by the hand of Moses and Aaron.

Unanswered prayer is always a problem. Can God, the all-powerful, desert his people? Job was given the answer, in the final chapters of his book, that we cannot presume to understand the ways of God. 'Have you ever in your life given orders to the morning or sent the dawn to its post?' (Job 38:12). The Suffering Servant in the poem of Isaiah 53 is sustained by the conviction that, in God's final triumph, not only will God triumph but he himself will be vindicated. God has his own way of managing things.

Psalm 77[78]: The lessons of history: a ballad

The first eight verses leave us in no doubt that this psalm is instructional. Like any good ballad, it teaches the lessons of history. It also has a ballad's repetitious quality. The 40 years of desert wanderings were regarded in two entirely different ways in Israel. In one way, they were seen as the honeymoon period of untarnished love, just after the marriage-alliance by which the Lord took Israel as his spouse – the period of bonding, when Israel was perfectly faithful to her spouse and the marriage-bond grew deeper. In another way, these years were seen as the period of budding rebellion and murmuring, foreshadowing the later growth of idolatry and fertility cults. In this ballad the latter mood prevails: again and again 'their hearts were not faithful to him', but still the Lord was full of compassion and forgiveness (vv. 9–41). Just as the later history of Israel is depicted, it is a repeated cycle of four movements: rebellion, punishment, repentance and forgiveness.

Then (vv. 42–53) the ballad turns back, rather unexpectedly, to the prelude that they had forgotten, the demonstration of the Lord's love for his people in the plagues he had inflicted on Egypt to force the Egyptians to release them. To the Hebrews, these were signs of the Lord's love; to the Egyptians, of his power. It is a different account of the plagues from that given in the book of Exodus – not ten but five, six or seven of them (depending on whether the two parallel halves of some verses describe the same or different plagues), but ending with the slaughter of the firstborn.

With the entry into Canaan, the same cycle of infidelity continues, climaxing in the total rejection of the north, which was to become the separatist kingdom of Israel. This rejection is focused on the destruction of the first sanctuary at Shiloh and the loss of the sacred ark of the covenant, the symbol of God's presence, to the Philistines. So searing was this tragedy that widows had no tears left for their menfolk who fell by the sword (v. 64), but here it is outdone by the even greater disaster, the destruction of Ephraim, the northern kingdom, and of its capital Samaria, in 721BC.

As a contrast, the ballad concludes with the divine choice of Judah, Zion and the line of David, the southern kingdom. The psalm must have been written between the sack of Samaria and the destruction, in its turn, of Jerusalem in 586BC – perhaps during the over-confident period of Josiah's reforms in 620. Later readers can only marvel at such complacency, especially since the cycle of rebellion and punishment was to continue. God's choice must evoke a corresponding response, whether the chosen ones are Jews or Christians.

Psalm 78[79]: The nations have invaded your heritage

Like Psalm 73[74], this prayer expresses the boiling over of anger and indignation at the destruction of Jerusalem and its temple. It could be about either the sack of Jerusalem by the Babylonians in 586BC or the assault on and desecration of the temple by the Syrian King Antiochus Epiphanes, four centuries later. A pronounced similarity to the language and thought of Jeremiah, who was present at the earlier destruction, may tip the balance in favour of the Babylonian period. At the time, this event seemed totally disastrous, the end of everything that the citizens of Jerusalem held dear.

There is perhaps enough about the present state of Jerusalem ('no one to bury the dead', v. 3) to suggest that the singer was one of those left behind amid the ruins. We do not know how total was the deportation to Babylon; there must have been enough citizens left behind to compose and sing the Lamentations in the ruins of the temple, as a skeletal shadow of the prescribed liturgy. They may even, as a sort of unreformed survival, have formed the core of the opposition to those who returned from Babylon two generations later, with all their new ideas of the spruced-up Judaism developed in Babylon. The cries for vengeance are strident and repeated: they are the violent overflow of burning anger. Christian ideals of forgiveness and 'turning the other cheek' have, as yet, no place in this spirituality.

More relevant is the call on God to protect the glory of his name (v. 9) and avenge the taunts uttered against him (v. 12). God's failure to protect his own people was taken as a sign of weakness by Israel's Gentile neighbours, and was an obvious reproach. The restoration of his people would re-establish his reputation, his Name. The petition in the Lord's Prayer that God's name be held holy is close in content, as well as position, to the prayer for the coming or total realisation of God's kingship. God would be king indeed when all people recognised the power of his name and paid it due homage, not only in words but also in deeds, system of values and way of life. Even after the return from exile, Judea remained so much the plaything of foreign powers, so tossed between one and another – Egypt, Syria and Rome – that the Jews never felt free of dominating powers, free to be God's own people. In addition, Jesus taught that the way in which they were setting about promoting God's rule and kingship was misdirected. A total change of direction was needed: 'Change your ways, for the kingdom of heaven is close at hand' (Matthew 3:2).

Psalm 79[80]: The vine of Israel

In this psalm, the title is verse 1.

Two great images, both important in the Old Testament and taken up in the New, dominate this psalm: the shepherd of Israel and the vine of Israel. As a whole, this psalm pairs with the previous one: as Psalm 78[79] prayed for the restoration of Jerusalem and the southern kingdom, so this prays for the restoration of the northern kingdom – Ephraim, Benjamin and Manasseh. Unusually, the might of God is to be roused not to destroy the enemies of Israel but (in a repeated refrain) to convert Israel and bring its people back. There is no questioning the justice of the punishment imposed, only how long it will last (v. 5).

First, God is the shepherd of Israel, who guides and guards his sheep, who 'leads Joseph [the northern territories] like a flock' (v. 2). In a daring transference, the image is applied in the New Testament to Jesus, thus suggesting his divinity. He takes pity on his people, who are 'like sheep without a shepherd', and then feeds them in pastures green near the restful waters of the lake of Galilee (Mark 6:34–44; Psalm 22[23]). The image is filled out in John 10, describing the good shepherd who gives his life for his sheep.

The central image in this psalm is the expansive vine of Israel, spreading over the awesome cedars of Lebanon and as far as the Great River, the Euphrates – as, theoretically, did the empire of David and Solomon. The image is used by Isaiah (ch. 5) in his complaint against the unfruitfulness of the vine of Israel, an image taken up in turn by Jesus, who directs it against the leaders, the wicked tenants who kill the prophets and the Son instead of yielding due payment to the owner of the vineyard (Mark 12:1–12).

A Christian reading of the psalm may go still further. The expression 'son of man' is twice used in the concluding verses as the focus of the vine and linked especially to God (vv. 16, 18). This expression, which in itself means no more than 'human being', was Jesus' favourite way of referring to himself. In the gospels, it also has the overtones of the glorious Son of Man in Daniel's vision (Daniel 7:13), who receives from the One of Great Age all authority over the universe. If we pray the psalm in the light of the New Testament, we may see a fuller sense of the son of man who brings us back so that we may 'never forsake you again' (v. 19).

Psalm 80[81]: Listen, my people!

In this psalm, the title is verse 1.

A noisy musical celebration starts this psalm. According to the parallelism of verse 4, the festivity seems to be both at the beginning and at the height of the month. Which feast-day? As the short historical psalm which follows celebrates the deliverance from Egypt, the feast-day may be Sukkoth ('Shelters'). This feast commemorates both the deliverance from Egypt ('I freed your shoulder from the builder's basket', v. 7) and the wanderings in the desert. It is still celebrated by living and feasting in the open, as far as possible, in shelters of branches outside the house, more or less mimicking life in the desert. In the psalm, however, the celebration soon gives way to more sombre memories of the times of disobedience in the desert.

It was at Meribah (the name means 'place of quarrelling') that Moses struck the rock twice (Numbers 20:11–12); this was construed as a moment of mistrust and cost him exclusion from the land of Canaan.

In contrast to this disobedience, a theme of the psalm is 'Listen, my people!' This idea occurs four times, in verses 9 (twice), 12 and 14. The rest of the psalm is a lament at the failure to follow this command, and a promise of victory and plenty for success in following it. The command reminds the Israelite of the key text of the covenant: 'Listen, Israel! The Lord our God is one Lord. And you shall love the Lord your God with all your heart, with all your soul, with all your strength' (Deuteronomy 6:4–5). This text, still part of the twice-daily prayer, used as the final prayer for children as they snuggle under the duvet, is to be 'fastened on your hand as a sign, on your forehead as a headband, on the doorposts of your house and on your gates' (Deuteronomy 6:8–9). That is, this command of the love of God above all things must dominate every aspect of life. To it Jesus himself, using a good principle of rabbinic exegesis, *gezerah shavah*, joins the second commandment, as equal to the first: 'And you shall love your neighbour as yourself' (Leviticus 19:18; Mark 12:30–31). (The seven principles of Jewish exegesis of the Bible were said to have been codified by Rabbi Hillel, a contemporary of Jesus. The principle of *gezerah shavah* is that if a phrase occurs twice in the Bible, the two occurrences should be understood in terms of each other. The phrase 'and you shall love' occurs only these two times in the Hebrew Bible.)

Psalm 81[82]: God stands in the divine assembly

Here we are confronted with very ancient beliefs. Central to the idea is that God was surrounded by a host of lesser gods. The same plural word, *elohim*, is used here for 'God' and 'gods'. While Israel initially believed that God was their only God, champion and protector, this did not exclude the possibility that other nations might have other gods, champions and protectors ('henotheism'). God, the Lord, could be worshipped only on the soil of Israel. So David, when he defected to the Philistines, could not worship the Lord in their territory. Similarly, Naaman, commander of the Syrian army, when cured of his leprosy by the prophet Elisha, took back to Syria three donkey-loads of soil from Israel, so that he could stand on them and worship the Lord (2 Kings 5:17). It was only when they were confronted by the host of Babylonian gods and goddesses during the exile that Israel advanced to monotheism – the belief that the Lord is God of the whole universe.

There are still traces in the Bible that the patrons of other cities and nations were somehow regarded as lesser deities. Eventually these beliefs were fused into the idea of angel-guardians. So the seven letters in Revelation 2—3 are written to the 'angels of the church' in Sardis, Ephesus, and so on. In Job 1—2, the 'sons of God', including Satan, the official tester of human beings, surround God as his holy court. In the development of thought, they eventually become angels, his servants, the powers of God who do his will. As a great king has a great court, with many ranks of courtiers, so God has a court of many angels of different ranks. Such angelology was in full development at the time of Jesus and in post-biblical Judaism.

The setting of this psalm is the heavenly court, and the divine beings are being condemned to death by God for their maladministration of justice – for not doing justice to the weak and the needy, the poor and the afflicted. Presumably these superior beings are seen as standing behind the human judges in their maladministration of justice. We are reminded of the parable of the unjust judge in Luke 18:1–8. The task of Israel, and especially of its judges, was to protect the weak and the needy as the Lord himself had protected Israel when they were weak and needy in Egypt. This is the meaning of the final appeal to God, the Lord and judge of all the world.

Psalm 82[83]: Let them seek your name, O Lord

In this psalm, the title is verse 1.

Israel was then, as now, surrounded by hostile tribes and nations. As Israel was God's chosen people, the psalmist's attitude was to identify hostility against Israel as hostility against God. At the beginning of this psalm the author insists, 'Your enemies hate you; they plot against your people.' At the end, his prayer is that 'they seek your name' and 'know that you alone are Most High'. The imprecations are, after all, a prayer, albeit a rather unsteady one, that the enemies may be converted rather than annihilated.

Reactions to exploitation by colonial systems and the genocides of the 20th century have made us aware of the interdependence of races and of a worldwide shared responsibility for one another. This awareness makes unacceptable the blinkered aggressiveness of the psalm and its unquestioned assumption that any attack on Israel is an attack on God, any offence against Israel an offence against God. At the same time, it is only fair to remember the traditional fraternal rivalry with Edom and Moab (v. 7) associated with the name of Ishmael (Abraham's son by the slave-girl Hagar), the repeated incursions of the Philistines (v. 8), and the marauding attacks of Midian (v. 10) and the Amalekites of David's time. The stories of Sisera and Jabin are told in the book of Judges, although the grisly details of bodies rotting on the ground escape us. The other princes recalled are also mentioned briefly in the same book.

As verse 5 declares, the existence of God's people had been threatened over the centuries, and the sensitivities of globalisation were still two millennia away. Even after the teachings of Jesus on forgiveness of enemies, his followers have practised hideous inhumanities in his name and continue to do so. Our reaction must be gratitude that our understanding of God's ways has advanced from those brutal times, coupled with repentance for our own personal hostilities and a prayer that we may come to a fuller appreciation of peace.

The psalm is neatly organised, with prayer for destruction of the enemies (vv. 2–5), followed by descriptions of military conflicts (vv. 6–13), three images of chaff in the fire, forest fire and tempest (vv. 14–16), and finally prayer that the enemies may acknowledge the Lord (vv. 17–19).

Psalm 83[84]: How lovely is your dwelling-place

In this psalm, the title is verse 1.

The tone is set for this appreciative and contented psalm by the reassuring image of the sparrow finding a home and the swallow a nest at the altar. It is a hymn of the welcome to God's house. We may most easily understand its structure in terms of the three blessings: 'Blessed are they who dwell in your house', 'Blessed are they whose hearts are set on pilgrimage', and 'Blessed is the one who trusts in you.' Thus the first blessing is on those who are actually in the courts of the Lord (vv. 2–5), the second on those who are on pilgrimage and striving to get there (vv. 6–11), and the third, more generally, on those who trust in the Lord (vv. 12–13). It is therefore a trio of widening circles, starting with the temple, God's dwelling-place in Jerusalem, and ending with those who worship everywhere 'in spirit and in truth', as Jesus said to the Samaritan woman (John 4:24).

Attempts were made in the 1960s to avoid the 'churchy' overtones of this frequent formula ('Blessed are they…') by translating it as 'Happy are…' or, more recently, as 'Congratulations to…!' Although such expressions are more familiar, they do not adequately reflect the meaning, which is strictly theological. It is nothing to do with the state of mind, contented or miserable, or with the achievements, praiseworthy or insignificant, of the person so described. The gospels do not pretend that the hungry and the thirsty are enjoying themselves! Rather, it means that God's caring hand is on them. Far from forgetting them, God's special care cherishes them and will ensure that they finally come to no harm but will enter into God's own blessedness.

The celebratory tone is strengthened by the triple designation of God as 'Lord of Hosts' (vv. 9, 10, 13). Although the word *sebaoth*, translated 'hosts', can be used of an earthly, military throng (1 Samuel 17:45), its typical use (and the use here most apt) is of the heavenly host, imagined as a throng of heavenly courtiers, angels or even sun and stars, surrounding the majestic throne of God. It is so used in the earliest prophetic description by Micaiah of God seated on his heavenly throne (1 Kings 22:19), a description that is further developed in Isaiah's vocation-vision of the Lord whose train fills the temple (Isaiah 6:1), then the magnificent vision of the chariot-throne of God in Ezekiel 1, and finally the description of the heavenly throne-room in Revelation 4—5.

Psalm 84[85]: Bring us back, O God, our Saviour!

In this psalm, the title is verse 1.

The psalm begins with an earnest – indeed, passionate – plea for God to withdraw his anger and bring Israel back to himself (vv. 2–8). Then comes the answer in the form of a divine promise of God's peace (vv. 9–14).

The first problem is to understand what is meant by God's anger. This is clearly an anthropomorphism, attributing human feelings to God. 'Anger', as we use the word, implies uncontrolled emotion, but God cannot lose his temper or be petulant. The cause of God's anger is always failure to observe the covenant. If the covenant is regarded as a marriage-covenant, such failure is analogous to infidelity in marriage, and God's 'anger' may be considered analogous to the explosive and justified anger of a spouse at the infidelity of a partner. On the other hand, since in God it is no irrational emotion but, rather, God's attitude to human infidelity, it may be better described by a different and unusual word: 'wrath'. God's wrath is there to be turned away by his mercy and by human repentance – turning back to God. In Paul's letters, especially in Romans, God's wrath and 'the day of wrath' is an eschatological element, the fate reserved for those who refuse to turn back to him. It is turned away by human trust in God's promises, fulfilled through the loving obedience of Christ, which annuls or washes away human disobedience. The Christian answer, then, to the questions in the first part of the psalm ('Will you be angry with us forever?') is that the wrath of God will be turned back by the perfect return of the second Adam, in the name of humanity, to perfect fidelity and obedience to God.

In the second half of the psalm, the sacred author speaks prophetically of the reconciliation. He is enabled to see, even then in a mysterious manner, that somehow the reconciliation will occur. The wonderful terms of the promise in verse 11, 'merciful love and faithfulness', are picked up by the prologue to the gospel of John (1:14, 17), translated 'grace and truth through Jesus Christ'. They are fulfilled in Jesus, through his incarnation and by his cross and resurrection. The 'faithfulness' which will spring from the earth is the fulfilment of the divine promises to Israel. The 'righteousness' which looks down from heaven is the perfect fulfilment of the Law, bringing perfect peace and harmony with God. Thus, at the end of time, is completed the 'salvation', and then 'his glory will dwell in our land'.

✓ Psalm 85[86]: Fear of the Lord

There is a special and attractive intimacy about this psalm. It could be regarded as an assemblage of quotations from other parts of the Bible and from other psalms, for it has not much originality, no straining for novelty. The relationship between psalmist and God is that of a loyal servant to the master: it begins and ends with the thought of the psalmist as 'your servant' (vv. 2, 16), and seven times God is referred to as 'my Lord'. God is also addressed directly as 'you, my God' or 'you, my Lord' several times. All this suggests the psalmist's affectionate attachment to God.

The structure of the psalm is woven round the central core to bring emphasis to its central element – verse 11, a plea from the psalmist that the Lord will unite or focus his heart in the Lord's way and in reverence for the Lord's name:

Verse 2: Your servant
    Verse 5: Full of mercy
        Verse 9: Glorify your name
            Verse 11: Focus my heart to fear your name
        Verse 12: Glorify your name
    Verse 15: Full of mercy
Verse 16: Your servant

It should strike us as odd that the psalmist centres his prayer on a plea for the gift of fear. However, fear of the Lord is the crown of the gifts that the Spirit will give to the Messiah (Isaiah 11:1–3). It is an element in the appreciation of the daunting majesty of the Holy One of Israel (Isaiah 6:1–5). The only due reaction to the approach of the Lord is to hide in the rocks 'in terror of the Lord, at the brilliance of his majesty, when he arises to make the earth quake' (Isaiah 2:19). This central plea is, then, the same as the plea of the Lord's Prayer, 'Hallowed be your name.'

Therefore, this prayer is balanced on either side by a prayer to 'glorify your name forever' (vv. 9, 12). A further balancing envelope is the mention of the favourite description of God in the Old Testament, as a God of mercy (vv. 5, 15). This is an allusion to the precious passage in Exodus 34:6 where God at last reveals the meaning of his special name, YHWH, too holy and too intimate to be pronounced. Such a tight pattern of envelopes within envelopes is not uncommon in Hebrew literature.

Psalm 86[87]: The gates of Zion

At the time of the Babylonian exile, the Jews became more conscious of other nations, their gods and their religious identity. With the return from exile they began to become more and more conscious that the vocation of Judaism was for all nations to draw salvation from Jerusalem. God had chosen them not for themselves alone but for the sake of others too. God's age-old promise to Abraham was framed, 'In you all nations will bless themselves' (Genesis 12:3). Jerusalem was the centre of salvation for the whole world, and all nations would stream to it. In the later part of Isaiah, this idea is joyfully expressed: 'The nations will come to your light, and kings to your dawning brightness' (60:3). Such universalism will find its fulfilment, though in the reverse direction, in the programme set out in Acts, as the good news is to spread by the apostles from Jerusalem to Judea and Samaria, and eventually to the remotest end of the earth (Acts 1:8). This is the glorious thing that is told of Zion (Psalm 86[87]:3).

The nations which have attacked and harmed Jerusalem are named in verse 4; even they will receive blessings from their association with Jerusalem. Rahab is properly the great sea-monster, but is also used as a name for Egypt, which was always ready to seize territory from Israel. The depradations of Babylon were obvious enough. In the early history of the settlement in Canaan, the encroachments of the Philistines were the chief threat. Ethiopia seems to be the furthest nation of which Israel took much notice: this is the importance of the Ethiopian official converted by Philip the deacon (Acts 8:26–40). All these nations will be counted as citizens of Jerusalem, included in its registers as though they had been born there, benefiting from the blessings given to it by the Lord.

Jerusalem had had a symbolic dimension since David made it God's capital (and his own) by bringing in the ark of the covenant. This symbolism is intensified by such writings as the detailed plans for the new and eschatological building of Jerusalem in the final chapters of Ezekiel. At the death of Jesus, Matthew depicts the sacred dead rising from their tombs and going into the holy city (27:53). The fullness of the vision is provided by the description of the new Jerusalem, the bride of the Lamb, in the final chapters of Revelation. The city will be lit by the radiant glory of God and the Lamb, and all nations will come to its light (Revelation 21:23–24).

Psalm 87[88]: Like a warrior without strength

In this psalm, the title is verse 1.

Most of those psalms which are tragic complaints about misfortune end up praising God for delivery from the misfortune. This meditation on a lonely, powerless death has no such redeeming feature. There seem to be no grounds for hope at all, although perhaps the very fact that the psalmist goes to the trouble of detailing such hopeless misery implies confidence that God can be persuaded to change it – or, at least, take a sympathetic interest. It is, in any case, a fine statement of a disaster situation and approaching death.

The psalm may be divided into three sections, each beginning with the plea that the psalmist cries out in prayer day and night (v. 2), or all day long (v. 10) or in the morning (v. 14). The first and the third complain about his utter lack of friends, with increasing intensity. In verse 9, 'acquaintances' are put at a distance from the psalmist; in verse 19 it is 'companions' and anyone who loves him.

The first section is dominated by two haunting military images. The lot of a heroic warrior who suddenly finds himself deserted by his strength, and powerless (v. 5), is very grim; it is almost a contradiction in terms, for the noun used for the fighter implies triumph. However, one roaming among the corpses of the dead (v. 6) is equally bitter. The second section consists of four sarcastic questions to God, suggesting that once the psalmist has made the impending small step into death, it will be too late for God to save him so that he can acknowledge and praise God. It is a sort of ultimatum! The third section is a random series of images of hopelessness.

There this tragic psalm ends, without a ray of comfort. The nearest approach to hope comes from the threats to God in the middle section, offering God, so to speak, a last chance to save the psalmist. This has been called the most desolate of all the psalms.

Psalm 88[89]: I will sing forever of your love, O Lord

In this psalm, the title is verse 1.

This psalm is at once both one of the most hopeful and one of the saddest of the psalms. It sets in contrast on the one hand God's love and fidelity and the promises announced to David, and on the other the failure of this promise. If God is loving and faithful, how can he have failed to fulfil his promise?

Seven times (the perfect number) in the course of the psalm, these two key qualities of God, love and faithfulness, are stressed in unison (vv. 2, 3, 15, 25, 29, 34, 50). *Hesed* is the indefectible family love which can be relied on above all things, especially in the close-knit Jewish family. The one rock of certainty is that home is always home, and family will never let you down. This is God's love for his family. And *'emet*, God's truth and fidelity (improbably from the same root as the familiar word 'Amen' – but don't even think of trying to understand Hebrew roots!), means 'firmness' and 'security'. If God is not reliable, there is no such thing as reliability. These are the basic pillars of all certainty and security.

Add to these the covenant with David, an intensification of the covenant with Moses. In the story of King David, when David offered to build the temple as a house for the Lord, the Lord replied with a promise: David was not to build a house for the Lord, but the Lord would build a House for David – that is, a dynasty that would last forever. Our psalm quotes this promise at length, and indeed this poetic version may well be older than the prose version given in 2 Samuel 7. The psalmist's problem is that, despite God's love and fidelity, the promise has not been kept: Israel has been dragged into exile, her king in chains and her monarchy shattered. Israel's consistent infidelity to the covenant, her flirting with other gods and her disregard of the poor, the weak and disadvantaged and all God's favourites, had left the Lord no alternative.

For the Christian, things look different. In the prologue to John's gospel we are reminded that the law came through Moses, but grace and truth – the same words, *hesed* and *'emet* – through Jesus Christ. It is in Christ that the promises of an eternal dynasty of the house of David are fulfilled. Do we turn our backs on this fulfilment just as determinedly as Israel turned her back on the covenant?

The psalm ends with a doxology, a couplet in praise of God. This is the ending not of this individual psalm, but of the third book of Psalms: compare Psalms 40[41] and 71[72].

Book 4

Psalm 89[90]: You sweep men away like a dream!

A meditation on time and eternity, this psalm sways between the stability of divine permanence and the instability of human life. Words for the passage of time abound: 'from age to age', 'a watch in the night', 'all our days', 'the span of our years', 'the number of our days', 'dawn' and 'the years when we looked upon evil'. All this reflection on the instability of human life contrasts with God's stability and the nearest approach to it that we know, the permanence of the mountains and the earth itself. In Palestine the grasses may be fresh and green in the morning but withered and brittle after a day scorched by the sun. In April the wild flowers and fruit blossoms are brilliant; by the end of May all is yellow and cracked by the heat.

At the opening of the poem, the author is keenly aware of the opening scenes of the Bible – creation and the Fall, with its penalty of death, the return to dust. The threefold mention of God's anger in verses 7–11 may give an impression that human instability is to be seen as a punishment for human sin, but there is much more emphasis on divine mercy, on wisdom of heart and on joy and success. These give the poem a mood of tranquillity and quiet rejoicing. There is no need to be afraid of the passage of time. The message is, then, perhaps one of contentment in the swirling changes and passage of human life, lived in the confidence of divine stability and divine care. All the circumstances of life may change but the Lord is still our refuge from generation to generation.

Seventy years, or 'eighty, if we are strong' (v. 10), is a generous reckoning of life expectancy in those days. Life was short and tough, with the ever-present threat of inexplicable and untreatable sickness, infertility, brigandage, injustice, famine and war. The immense ages ascribed by the Bible to the patriarchs of old are not to be taken literally. They are more signs of special divine blessing, enabling the founder figures to escape for a little longer the even grimmer fate of being simply dissolved back into the family stem. Nevertheless, the prayer ends in this psalm on the relaxed note of a double plea for success.

Psalm 90[91]: He who dwells in the shelter of the Most High

For the Christian reader, the clue to the understanding of this psalm is given by its quotation by the Tempter ('Satan' means 'the Tempter' or 'Tester') in the story of Jesus' testing (Matthew 4:6). Jesus is in the desert after his baptism, working out what form his messianic mission should take. In the end, after the Tempter has put forward three false alternatives, Jesus sees that his mission is to be the suffering servant of the Lord. Meanwhile, however, three times the Tempter flaunts the scripture in front of Jesus, and each time Jesus replies with another text which shows that he has more control and understanding of the meaning of scripture than the Tester himself.

In the second test, the Tempter quotes sarcastically from today's psalm ('They shall bear you up on their hands lest you strike your foot against a stone') to voice the suggestion that Jesus thinks himself so close to God that he can come to no harm. Jesus replies with a quotation from Deuteronomy 6:16: 'You shall not put the Lord your God to the test.'

Yes, the Tester is right (there is always *some* attractive truth in the devil's suggestions) that the psalm meditates warmly and intimately on God's care and protection of one who puts full trust in the Most High. This is expressed in a lovely series of paired images running throughout the psalm as it details the dangers from which God will protect: the trickery of snares, terrors of the dark, human violence, sickness, wild animals, and possibly a mythical dragon. Hebrew poetry in general, and the psalms in particular, derive their balance from such repetitious parallelism, but in this case the tranquillity imparted is especially satisfying: shelter and shade, refuge and stronghold, snare and plague, pinions and wings, buckler and shield, and so on. Occasionally there is an even closer, reversing link: clings in love – free – protect – knows my name (v. 14). In the monastic prayer of the Church, this psalm is prayed every evening at the final prayer of Compline, as the monk securely and contentedly yields himself into the care of God for the night.

Psalm 91[92]: It is good to give thanks to the Lord

In this psalm, the title is verse 1.

The headings or titles of each psalm in the Bible were added later and are not part of the original psalms. At the head of this psalm stands a liturgical note: 'A song for the Sabbath'. It has been suggested that this ascription may come from the fact that the sacred name 'the Lord' occurs in the psalm seven times, the perfect number.

Whether or not this is the case, it is valuable to reflect on this mysterious name, which in Judaism is never pronounced. A superficial reason for this is that we do not know how it was pronounced. In classical Hebrew, only the consonants are written – in this case 'YHWH'. At one stage, the word was turned into English as 'Jehovah', which is quite certainly incorrect. When the Four Letters occurred in the Hebrew text, the reader would read out 'Adonai', and eventually the vowels of 'Adonai' were married to the consonants of 'YHWH' to produce the misbegotten word 'Jehovah'.

The deeper reason, however, is that the name is both too intimate and too awesome to be spoken. It is not the common word for God or gods, but is the special name of the God of Israel. Each of us has a special, intimate family name, a term of endearment, often embarrassing but always a sign of deep love in the family and certainly not to be spoken to strangers. So YHWH lies too deep in the heart to be used aloud.

The word is also too awesome. It was revealed to Moses at the burning bush (Exodus 3:1–15). To reveal your name is a sign of friendship and trust. Once someone possesses your name, they can begin to unlock your secrets, to 'steal your identity'. The name was given to Moses as an assurance of God's patronage as he stood before Pharaoh, but no meaning was given on that occasion. When Moses asked the meaning, he was told merely 'I am who I am'. It was only later, when Israel had sinned and smashed the brand new alliance with God, that God revealed the meaning of the name. God passed before Moses, crying out, 'YHWH, YHWH, God of tenderness and compassion, slow to anger, rich in faithful love' (Exodus 34:6). This was the meaning and concept of their God which echoed down to the scriptures of Judaism – a God of loving forgiveness.

Psalm 92[93]: Greater than the roar of mighty waters

This is the first of a group of psalms celebrating the kingship of the Lord, comprising also Psalms 94—98[95—99]. Most of them include the refrain 'The Lord is King!' which can also be translated 'The Lord *has become* King'. For some years in the last century, it was strongly held that this cry indicated a festival celebrating the renewal of the kingship of the Lord. Such an annual festival existed in other Near Eastern countries, but it is difficult to believe that it was celebrated in Israel, since there is no explicit trace of it in the Bible and in the full instructions about festivals given there. It is also difficult to envisage, for Israel, the notion of God ever ceasing to be king, that his kingship should be renewed. In recent years the thesis has largely waned.

This psalm is among the oldest in the collection and probably dates from the very earliest times in Canaan. Baal, the chief Canaanite god, was a god of storm and the powers of nature, and the same imagery is applied here to the Lord. There is also the rhythm of early Canaanite poetry, most clearly visible in verse 3: one line of two elements, followed by a line in which a third is added: 'the rivers have lifted up, the rivers have lifted up *their voice*.'

In the early imagery of the Bible, water is rightly conceived as a mighty and terrifying force. As the chaos and death wreaked by a tsunami show, no natural weather phenomenon is as powerful. In addition, the Hebrew picture of primitive chaos is of a limitless mass of waters. God divides the waters to insert the world – a flat plate, covered by a dome, with sluice-gates in the dome to admit the rain – and then continues to hold back the waters. If, at any moment of his continuing act of creation, God were to withdraw this restraint on the waters, they would rush together again and the world would implode, leaving only the formless mass of waters.

A further element in the imagery is perhaps the sound-play of the central verses. The Hebrew of verse 3, about the rivers, is dominated by a gentle *n* consonant, perhaps expressing the smooth-flowing waters, while verse 4, dominated by final *-im*, *-am*, *-om*, may render the booming of the waves of the sea. All of these seek to express the kingship of God over the natural forces of the world.

Psalm 93[94]: Avenging God, shine forth!

The 'envelope' of this psalm, the first and last verses, concentrates on vengeance – not the most Christian of motifs. One of the great advances of Jesus' teaching in the Sermon on the Mount was the replacement of even the limited vengeance allowed by ancient law-codes and Mosaic legislation with the teaching on turning the other cheek. Within this envelope, however, comes a prayer of confidence that the Lord will not allow the persecution of those who trust in him to continue unheeded.

This provides us with a useful recognition of the universal human instinct of crying for vengeance. It cannot be disguised or neglected. Our automatic reaction to hurt is always to hurt back, to repay injury with injury, as though this promotes justice. Just as 'one good turn deserves another', so we assume that one bad turn deserves another. Does the principle of balance really apply in this case? Does the hurt inflicted in recompense for a hurt really restore a balance or merely provide a jumping-off point for a new spiral of injury? We can be misled by the image of the scales of justice, neatly balanced. The long-running individual and national feuds of history are enough to show that such a balance is no road to peace, whether the sphere is Northern Ireland, Israel, Rwanda or the long-running family feud. The spiral of tit-for-tat continues until the stronger of the two parties achieves the generosity of forgiveness. 'Blessed are the peacemakers' goes against every human instinct but, nevertheless, makes sense. Is it ever possible, though, without the strength that comes from God? It is one thing to reject the short-sighted model that one hurt somehow balances out another, but quite another thing to have the strength to put the alternative into practice. In Matthew's parable of the unforgiving servant (18:23–35), it takes the divine strength of the master of the servants to remit the inconceivably large debt. A similar model of forgiveness is simply beyond the conception of the escaping servant as he throttles his fellow worker.

The other aspect of the psalm is confidence that God sees and pays heed to injustice. We cannot blind ourselves to the fact that injustice is done, but we can turn to the Lord and accept that he who made the eye does indeed see, and invoke the mystery of suffering, again from the Beatitudes, 'Blessed are you when people persecute you on my account' (Matthew 5:11).

Psalm 94[95]: O that today you would listen to his voice

The similarity of this psalm to Psalm 80[81] is striking: both are divided into two parts, the first part being an invitation to come and worship, the second a reminiscence of the scenes of the exodus from Egypt and Israel's rebellions during that journey. It is almost as though both psalms were intended for the same liturgical shape of festival, although no festival is known which demands this style of liturgy.

The first seven verses constitute a call to approach for worship, bringing to mind the creative power of the Lord. These verses could form a processional song, leading up to an act of worship, kneeling in the temple. In many arrangements for monastic and other daily prayer, this psalm has indeed been used as the invitation to prayer at the beginning of the day.

The second half of the psalm harks back to a greater procession, the journey through the desert. It ends unsatisfactorily, as though cut short by God's oath that that generation would never enter his rest. However, a Christian view of these verses must be coloured by the use of the psalm in the letter to the Hebrews. Hebrews 4:1-11 links the divine mention of 'my rest' at the end of the psalm with the repose of God on the seventh day at the end of creation. This divine repose is seen as the goal of our own journeying too, 'a seventh-day rest reserved for God's people'. 'Massah' (v. 8) means 'trial' or 'testing', and 'Meribah' means ' place of strife or judgment', for it was there that the people rebelled at the lack of water, until Moses appealed to God and struck the rock from which water flowed (Exodus 17:1-7). By their refusal to trust God, the people of the desert were denied the possibility of entering this rest. So God fixed a new 'today' to which Christians are still pressing forward on pilgrimage.

Christ, the supreme high priest, has already gone through to the highest heaven and Christians are to follow him in approaching the throne of grace to receive mercy and blessing. This theology of a journey is the foundation of the rich idea that the church is a pilgrim church, a church of sinners, still imperfect and still pressing forward to its goal. Each morning with this prayer the pilgrimage begins anew or takes one more step forward.

Psalm 95[96]: Sing a new song to the Lord

It is possible to regard this psalm as having been artistically and artificially put together from a series of other psalms and hymns. Almost every line has its parallel elsewhere; details are given in the marginal references of some Bibles. This can be called the antho-logical style, as though flowers were picked from elsewhere and put together here to form a special bouquet. Then, again, it may all have been reused, for a very similar hymn is assigned to the Levites in the account of the transporting of the ark of the covenant to Jerusalem in 1 Chronicles 16:23–33. This suggests that the psalm was in use liturgically at the time when 1 Chronicles was written – that is, in the second century BC. This is, however, far from the suggestion that the psalm is secondary, let alone second-rate. It could also be that the author or authors used the common vocabulary of worship at the time.

In any case, the psalm carries two particularly strong impressions of Deutero-Isaiah, who prophesied in Babylon just before the end of the exile. One is the second stanza (vv. 4–6), which insists on strict monotheism, just as Deutero-Isaiah insistently maintains the purity of monotheism in the face of the many gods of Babylon (see, for example, Isaiah 44:6–20; 45:20–25). The other is the climax in the establishment of righteousness on earth, to which the final stanza leads (vv. 11–13), as does Isaiah 42:1–4. This 'righteousness' is sometimes translated as 'justice', but this is an impoverishment of the biblical concept. It is not justice in the sense of the treatment deserved by human, often sinful, action. God's righteousness is a saving justice. It does not consist in handing out due penalties and rewarding worthy behaviour. On the contrary, it is a forgiving justice that positively *makes* righteous any who turn to the Lord, and establishes peace and harmony on earth, despite human sin. As in verse 13, it is often allied to, and set in parallel with, God's truth, for in it God is being true to his promises, true to his nature as a forgiving

God, fulfilling his covenant with Abraham and with his chosen people. So it is possible to pray, 'In your righteousness/justice set me free', not as a protestation of innocence but as an appeal for divine forgiveness. For Paul (in Romans 4), it is the righteousness given to Abraham not as a reward for any conduct of his own but simply because he trusted in God.

Psalm 96[97]: The Lord is king, let earth rejoice

The prevailing imagery for the Lord in this psalm is light. There is a gradual progression. At the beginning we see only the sombre cloud and darkness around him, then a fire 'walks before him' (v. 3). His lightnings break forth to lighten the world. Their power is seen as the mountains melt like wax. Then (v. 6) the light spreads to the skies to proclaim his righteousness. The same imagery of light reappears in the final verses, as light shines forth for the righteous (v. 11).

In the Bible, light has always been a symbol of God, seen in the rainbow that symbolised God's renewed favour after the destruction brought by the flood, and in the lightning that showed God's presence on Mount Sinai, the brightness associated with the glory of God on the mountain and reflected on the face of Moses. Most of all, we see it in the brilliant light all round the figure in Ezekiel's vision of the glory of God's throne (Ezekiel 1:27–28).

Light, warmth and growth are associated with one another. The sun and light signify especially the beneficent presence of God, and nowhere more so than in Isaiah: a light shining in the darkness (9:2), or the eschatological splendour of Jerusalem in Isaiah 60, 'Arise, shine, for your light is come', where the light attracts the nations to the salvation offered to them at Jerusalem. In the New Testament, this imagery of light is transferred to Jesus: the glory of the Lord 'shines' round the shepherds at the birth of Jesus, and his garments are suffused with light at the transfiguration, signifying his divine state. So the Word incarnate is the light coming into the world (John 1:9), which some accept and some reject, and part of Jesus' divine claim is 'I am the light of the world' (John 8:12).

At the same time, the real glory of God, proclaimed by the skies (v. 6), is his righteousness, his saving justice which 'righteouses' sinners – that is, makes sinners righteous. This is the aspect of God's kingship celebrated in this psalm, that he brings sinners together in his kingdom of holiness and righteousness.

Psalm 97[98]: All the ends of the earth have seen salvation

The striking feature of this psalm is its concern for the whole world. It shares with the psalms around it the same motifs of praise for the kingship of God, God's saving justice, his merciful family love for the house of Israel and his fidelity to his promises. The distinguishing feature, however, is the spread of all these qualities to the world as a whole. He has revealed his salvation in the sight of all nations (v. 2). All the ends of the earth have seen the salvation of our God (v. 3). All who dwell in the world acknowledge him (v. 7). He will judge the world and its peoples (v. 9). So often, we think of Judaism as a closed religion, concerned with its own members' election as the chosen people and hostile to outsiders.

Jesus himself had little contact with non-Jews: in the gospel of Mark we read of only one meeting with a Gentile, the Syro-Phoenician woman, whom he provokes to explicit faith by calling her a 'dog' (7:27). In John, the Gentiles make a roundabout approach to Jesus through one of the Twelve who happened to live on the borders of Galilee (John 12:20–21). At Pentecost there were present in Jerusalem representatives from all the nations around, but all were Jews. The events at Pentecost were followed by a great deal of hesitation over whether non-Jews could be received into the community of Christ's followers, and more hesitation about whether they must observe the Jewish law if they were received. Not until the letter to the Ephesians does the apostle teach that Christ has abolished the wall of separation to create in Christ a single new humanity from Jews and Gentiles (Ephesians 2:15).

It is almost as though a step backwards had been taken since the writing of our psalm, with its joyful celebration that 'all the ends of the earth' have seen the salvation of our God (v. 3) – the very expression used by the risen Lord to the apostles at the ascension. Yet from the exile onwards, the prophets are very conscious of the mission of Israel to bring salvation to the whole world. In dramatic contrast to the pre-exilic self-awareness of Israel and its separation from all other nations, the latest chapters of Isaiah are full of nations making their pilgrimage to Jerusalem to 'draw water from the springs of salvation' (12:3), sons and daughters coming from 'far away' to acknowledge the glory of the Lord (60:1–7). This was the beginning of the fulfilment of the promise to Abraham that all nations would 'bless themselves' in his name (Genesis 12:1–3).

Psalm 98[99]: The Lord is king; the peoples tremble

It is not easy to discern the exact structure of this psalm, the last of this group of psalms celebrating the Lord as king. It falls into three sections, ending 'Holy is he' (v. 3), 'Holy is he' (v. 5), and 'Holy is the Lord our God' (v. 9) respectively. So it is basically about God as the holy king. Another emphasis in Hebrew is rather less obvious in English – the elevated position of God on high: 'God is exalted above all the peoples' (v. 2) and 'exalt the Lord our God' (vv. 5, 9), the same verb being used in each case.

This psalm is not about temporal dignity or worldly acclaim or power, but uniquely about that awesome, frightening but attractive quality of holiness. About this divine quality Augustine says, '*ardesco et inhorresco*', perhaps to be translated, 'I burn with ardour but I recoil in dread.' To the holiness of God any human being is inescapably drawn; yet so dauntingly far is it above our experience that we cannot but shrink away in awe. At his experience of it in the temple, the confident Isaiah could only shrink away in terror at his own uncleanness (6:5). In another poem (2:6–22) he cries out repeatedly, 'Go into the rock, hide in the dust, in terror of the Lord, at the brilliance of his majesty, when he arises to make the earth quake.'

The holiness of God is not something to be trifled with. Even as experienced – rarely – in holy people, it attracts and it daunts us as something wonderful, uncontrollable, beyond our ken, and overwhelming. Moses was told, 'You cannot see God and live', and even what he did see of the glory of God left his face so calloused and scarred that he had to wear a veil (Exodus 34:35). In John 1:14, that was the daunting quality of Christ – 'We saw his glory, the glory that he has from the Father' – and at the marriage feast at Cana it is simply said, 'He revealed his glory, and his disciples believed in him' (2:11). In some way the glory of God was made visible and could be experienced in Jesus.

This is the exaltation, beyond the level of this world, and the holiness of God which is celebrated in the kingship of God in this psalm.

Psalm 99[100]: 'The Old Hundredth': a song of joyful praise

Although there is no mention in this psalm of the kingship of Yahweh, it conveniently closes the series of psalms celebrating that kingship. It is the last of a group of psalms of pure praise – that is, not attached to any particular circumstances. All we can deduce is that the psalm was obviously designed to be sung at the approach and entry to the sanctuary, while the singers 'entered his gates with thanksgiving'. The initial 'Cry out' denotes a certain exaltation, a shout of triumph. The Hebrew word is used of sounding the trumpets for victory, as at the taking of Jericho by Joshua (Joshua 6:5, 10, 16, 20). However, we must remember that trumpets in those days were not our brass instruments; they were the much gentler rams' horns. So, at the coming of the humble king in Zechariah 9:9, the daughters of Jerusalem are bidden to rejoice with the same sound. In some Christian traditions, this psalm serves instead of the Benedictus as the final canticle of morning prayer, but it is also redolent with the quiet exaltation of spirit that Mary expresses in her Magnificat.

The psalm is rich in the favourite imagery of the psalmists, as valid for Christians as it was for the original authors:

- Universalism (v. 1): the call to praise is addressed to 'all the earth', not just to Israel. This suggests that the psalm was part of the liturgy of the second, post-exilic, temple.
- The Lord as the shepherd of his flock (v. 3).
- The two bases of our reliance on God (v. 5). However much we fail and 'mess up', once we have finally been convinced that we cannot rely on ourselves we can rely on God's *hesed*, his motherly or fatherly love, and his *'emunah*, his fidelity to his promises.

The middle line of verse 3 presents an interesting little problem: the same written Hebrew word can be read out with two different meanings, so that two translations are possible (just as, in English, the word 'read' can be either present or past, pronounced 'reed' or 'red') – either 'He made us and *not we* (ourselves)' or 'He made us and *we* (belong) *to him*'. The translators of the Old Testament into Greek chose the former version, and of course the Greek version rather than the Hebrew was the Bible used by the Church for the first four centuries. The later rabbinic tradition chose the latter. The written text must have been understood in both ways at different times and different places.

Psalm 100[101]: I sing of love and justice

This is a Wisdom psalm, reflecting on the qualities and way of life that are the aim of a life well ordered. It would be entirely mistaken to dismiss it as boastful or arrogant, proclaiming the singer's own achievements and qualities, although we must admit that the reticence and modesty demanded by our age have no place in biblical thought. So the apostle Paul can say, 'Be imitators of me, as I am of Christ' (1 Corinthians 11:1). Nor is it useful to describe the hymn simply as a series of good resolutions.

The psalm should be read and prayed as a reflection on the divine qualities described, and a plea for them. It is, after all, addressed to God. It begins with a reflection on two salient qualities of God's dealings with his creation. God's *hesed* (love) gives us hope in despair and failure. We need not rely on our own achievements, our own strength or abilities, our own righteousness. *Hesed* makes home and family a source of reliance and refuge, the quality that every child (young or less young) seeks in a mother and a brother or sister. There, if nowhere else, the failure and the sinner can expect a welcome and forgiveness. In our dire need, a mother's sternness and a sibling's rivalry fall away, to leave raw and open the welcome and sympathy needed by a failure. Moses experienced this forgiving love (in Exodus 34:6) when, after Israel's blatant idolatry, the Lord defined himself as full of tenderness and compassion, rich in *hesed*. Ever since then, we have relied on this as the defining quality of God.

The other quality hymned by the psalmist in the first line is 'judgment' (NJB). This means God's decisions or verdicts, as in a law court. Usually God's *hesed* is paired with *'emet* or 'truth, trustworthiness'. Here it is more about the decisions that emanate from this quality than the quality itself. Verse 2 twice uses the word that means 'complete, blameless'. Rather than wanting to escape from due blame, the psalmist is praying for a fulfilled life, for completion and satisfaction, that God's decision will go the right way. If we believe in divine guidance, there is no such thing as 'luck'. A prayer that God's decisions may be complete, and that the psalmist may live a fulfilled life, is the believer's equivalent to wishing for good luck.

Psalm 101[102]: Do not hide your face from me!

In this psalm, the title is verse 1.

The logic and thrust of this psalm are not immediately clear. The early and late parts of the psalm (vv. 2–12 and 24–29) seem to be the lament or complaint of someone who is grievously sick and slipping towards death, while the central part (vv. 13–23) is a hymn of praise to the Lord in expectation of the re-establishment of the primacy of Jerusalem after the exile. So distinct are these two parts that they are often thought to be separate compositions, clumsily combined.

The clue to the unity of the composition is in verses 3 and 29, which bracket the psalm. Each refers to 'your face', although in verse 29 this is often translated 'your presence' or simply 'before you'. In fact, the expression used is 'before your face'. In each, the issue is the confrontation of the psalmist with the Lord – a saving confrontation that brings assurance and serenity. This is the theme of the psalm, at the beginning a plea not to withdraw this presence, and at the end a peaceful repose in that presence. Amid all the horrors so vividly pictured in the early section (withering like cut grass in the hot Palestinian sun, and those three lonely birds in verses 7–8), the psalmist is confident of the salvation brought by the benign face of the Lord.

What, then, does the central part contribute to this theme? The re-establishment of Jerusalem after the exile is used as a metaphor for the re-establishment of the psalmist after this dire sickness. If the

Lord can and will set up Jerusalem once more to be at the head of the nations and receiving their homage, he can and will also restore the psalmist.

The most intense and exciting section of the psalm is, however, the final one. There, the emphasis is on the transitory nature of the world: the heavens and the earth will perish, they will be changed, like a worn-out garment. And yet the Lord will be the same, and with him will be the psalmist, secure in his presence. At this stage of revelation, the final resurrection of the dead had not yet come into Israel's consciousness. There is, however, a proclamation of the belief that, when all is changed, when the universe itself has come to an end, God's faithful people will still be in the divine presence, standing before the face of the Lord.

Psalm 102[103]: The Lord forgives all your sins

One could say that the whole psalter is a song of praise to the saving justice of God. That is certainly true of this psalm. It circles round the three ideas of forgiveness, loving mercy (*hesed*, considered in our commentary a couple of psalms ago) and saving justice. These are the three aspects of God that are revealed as the Name of God in Exodus 34, which make Israel cling doggedly to God.

Saving justice was considered extensively in the commentary on Psalm 7, but there is room for more! There is no concept in English that adequately renders this aspect of God. For lack of a better word, it is sometimes rendered 'righteousness', which at any rate shows that there is no normal English word for it, though it has the disadvantage of smelling of 'self-righteousness' – not an amiable quality. The reflection on Psalm 7 centred on God's own righteousness – that is, God's absolute fidelity to his promises, the ground of all human hope. What about human righteousness?

In the New Testament, the paradigm cases come in the infancy narratives. In Matthew 1:19, Joseph is called 'righteous'. In Luke's infancy narrative, all the principal actors are 'righteous': the parents of John the Baptist, Simeon and the parents of Jesus are equally eager to obey the law to the letter (Luke 1:6; 2:22–25). They are being shown to us as the final spearhead of the faithful of the Old Testament, putting all their trust in God and all their hope in the coming of his Messiah. Their guiding principle in life is to stay close to God's law, for to obey the law is a loving response to God's gift of his revelation and friendship in the law. The law shows human beings how to stay close to God, how to be God's people, living in the image of God. So, just as God's 'righteousness' is his fidelity to his promises made to Abraham, so human 'righteousness' is fidelity to God's way of life, revealed in the law. It is not a 'hard' concept, like 'self-righteousness' or 'zeal', but is a 'soft' concept, a gentle and generous concept of self-giving. One is tempted to translate it as 'devotedness'. The parents of John the Baptist and of Jesus, and all who were ready to welcome the Messiah, were devoted.

In praising the 'righteousness' of God, then, we pronounce our reliance on God's fidelity to his promises and yearn to be, ourselves, faithful to the gift of his guidance.

Psalm 103[104]: Wrapped in light as in a garment

This is possibly the favourite of the creation psalms, rivalling Psalm 8 as the most beloved of the hymns of praise for the wonders and intricacy of God's creation. It shares many features and even verses with the Egyptian 'Hymn to Creation' (or 'Hymn to the Sun') attributed to Pharaoh Akhenaton, though direct borrowing in either direction is difficult to establish. It rejoices in the beauty and variety of created nature, including (vv. 16–18) such wonderful local features as the majestic cedars of Lebanon towering from the mountains, the delicate ibex or mountain goats (they blend so perfectly into the sandy rock of the wadis that they pass unnoticed till a stone is dislodged and tinkles down the slope) and the timid but inquisitive hyrax or 'rock rabbits' (not rabbits at all, but small, tailless, beaver-like creatures that bask in the sun and scuttle for safety in the rocks). Equal attention is paid to the young lions, who wait for darkness before they creep forth and roar for their prey, seeking their food from God (v. 21).

The series follows the order of the first creation narrative in Genesis 1 – a logical ordering, never intended as an historical, day-by-day account. First comes the framework – the light and the heavens – next the solid earth (v. 5), the springs of water that penetrate it from below and the rains from above (v. 10). Then come the moving things in the sky (v. 12), on earth (v. 20) and in the sea (v. 25), even the sea monsters which the Lord made to play with (v. 26).

The psalm concludes, as it began, with the praise of the Lord, leading the theme back to the beginning of the creation with the glory of the Lord, who is clothed in majesty. It has been suggested that Genesis 1 is a hymn to the one Creator, deliberately countering ideas that sun, moon and stars are gods in their own right: they are all the creatures of one God, planted by God in the heavens. In this psalm, too, sun and moon have their function within God's creation: the moon is merely a marker for feast days, and even the sun knows the time prescribed for its setting (v. 19). The psalm combines a reverence and affection for the things of earth with overwhelming praise for the Creator of them all.

Psalm 104[105]: Make known his deeds among the peoples

There are two striking aspects to this historical psalm. The first is that there is no hint of the disobedience of Israel or the corrections meted out by God; the second is that it is centred on the covenant, not with Moses but with Abraham.

Most of the historical psalms are well aware of the chequered history of Israel's fidelity to God. So Psalm 77[78] presents Israel as 'a defiant and rebellious race' constantly rebelling and deserting the Lord throughout its history. Psalm 105[106] dwells on Israel's forgetfulness and idolatry. Not so Psalm 104[105], for all is calm and peaceful here. Joseph is merely the successful precursor of the chosen people going into Egypt. The oppression in Egypt is mentioned only to explain the plagues. Of these, a luscious account is given, considerably different from the account in Exodus, though the psalm's poetic form makes it hard to discern whether the underlying historical facts were different. The journey through the desert sees every desire of Israel fulfilled. At every step, the Lord is arranging history to Israel's advantage, to which Israel responds blamelessly. Water from the rock, manna and quails are all answers to Israel's prayers.

Secondly, the central figure is Abraham at both beginning and end (vv. 6, 9, 42). Normally, 'the covenant' immediately evokes the covenant made with Moses during the exodus, but here (as in Paul's meditation on Abraham's faith in Romans 4) the emphasis is on the ultimate father of the race. The return to the promised land is seen as the fulfilment of the promises made to him in Genesis 12. Not surprisingly, after this smooth and harmonious account of the partnership between God and Israel, the purpose of the whole history is delineated as the observance of God's precepts and laws (v. 45).

The stress on instruction, wisdom and the law shows that this is a Wisdom psalm, and should be regarded not only as a song of praise for God's direction of history in favour of Israel but also as a means of instruction. This makes it all the more remarkable: Wisdom literature dates from a late period in the history of Israel, and yet the singer of this psalm takes one small segment of the history of Israel, seeing in it God's benevolent conduct of Israel's history and Israel's unhesitating obedience.

Psalm 105[106]: Visit me with your saving power

This is the last psalm of Book Four, so the final verse should be seen as a doxology not to the psalm but to the whole book – as at the end of each of the five books. The psalm was no doubt put here as a companion to the previous psalm, teaching in a complementary way the lessons of God's actions in history.

Indeed, it stands in sharp contrast to the previous psalm. There Israel was quietly cooperative with the Lord; here the repeated rebellion of Israel is foremost. So the psalm begins and ends with praise of God, but it is the praise of God's forgiveness and mercy, his *hesed*, despite Israel's rebelliousness. Despite the threats of enemies and the infidelity of Israel, God is a God who saves, for God is a Saviour-God, and it is only in the course of the development of Christology that the title of Saviour is transferred to our Lord and Saviour, Jesus Christ.

There are two sharply distinct ways of looking at the Israelites' 40 years in the desert. One is as the ideal time of the honeymoon between Israel and her Lord, a time of peace and fidelity, an idyll of untrammelled love. We see this affection portrayed in Hosea 11:1–4: 'I called my son out of Egypt… I was leading them… with leading-strings of love… I was like someone lifting an infant to his cheek.' Jeremiah speaks of 'the affection of your bridal days' (Jeremiah 2:2). Another viewpoint is represented by this psalm – the continual complaint and murmuring of the people as they worked their way through that inhospitable desert; their failure to understand the wonderful deeds of God in Egypt; their defiance at the Red Sea; their impatience, greed and challenge to God in the desert; their disbelief in God's guarantee of a land; their provocation to God at Meribah and their refusal to destroy the non-Yahwistic inhabitants of Canaan.

The desert of Sinai is indeed a testing place. Nothing grows in those vast expanses of harsh and unyielding sand. Of water, life and movement, there is nothing. Even the wild camels are panting in the merciless sun. To be lost on Sinai, as bewilderment passes to fear and frustration, is an experience that can still chill the heart years later. And yet, in this country of extremes, the brooding, unseen, almighty power of God is dauntingly present.

Book 5

Psalm 106[107]: Rescued by the Lord

The structure of this psalm is beautifully neat and tidy. The three-verse introduction begins with the favourite reminder of the everlasting mercy of the Lord, before acclaiming his mercy in bringing together a people from the four corners of the world. What is this 'gathering' that is described in verse 3? The date of the psalm makes little difference to its meaning and impact. In the post-exilic era there were three pilgrimage festivals in the year, and the psalm could refer to any of these gatherings, witnessing to the redemptive power of the Lord.

There follows the first main part of the psalm, which is composed of four neat and graphic sections on rescues from impending disasters, each with a parallel structure: a succinct and vivid description of the disastrous need, the cry for help, the rescue and the thanksgiving. In each, the desperate situation is sketched in a few well-chosen and deft strokes. The first describes one of the basic terrifying biblical experiences, and the desperate cry for help in a situation where there is no hope (vv. 4–9): no one who has not been lost in the desert can really understand the world of the Bible. The second plunges into the filth, darkness and chains of primitive imprisonment (none of the humanitarian mitigations of the modern prison here) and the release for which there is no hope (vv. 10–16). The third vividly describes the powerless loathing of the sick (vv. 17–22). While it is being suffered, any illness seems irremediable and hopeless! The fourth (vv. 23–32) confronts the mighty power of the sea, with people being tossed around in a cockleshell boat. The people of the Bible were not natural seafarers, and their fear of the sea was intensified by their mental image of the earth, tucked into the middle of raging waters that threatened to engulf the whole if God should for a moment cease to restrain them. This fourth rescue leads not merely to a prayer of thanks but to a public thanksgiving in the open assembly.

These detailed rescue operations by the Lord are followed by a more generalised reflection (vv. 33–42) on God's habit of reversing situations – what might be called by Christians 'the Magnificat syndrome' – the power to humble the proud and exalt the lowly. This is imaginatively focused on the disconsolate prince, wandering alone in trackless wastes, contrasted with the rescued needy, gleefully tucked up at home, surrounded by a family as numerous as a flock.

Psalm 107[108]: 'My heart is ready'

In this psalm, the title is verse 1.

The combination of parts of two other psalms creates a new prayer. This psalm is composed of Psalm 56[57]:8–11 followed by Psalm 59[60]:4–12. Each half of the psalm is torn from its context of a threatened situation and joined to the other, to make an altogether cheerful and positive hymn of praise.

Psalm 108[109]: A curse of curses

An occasional prayer for vengeance occurs in several psalms, but never anything so sustained and prolonged as the curse in this psalm. Attempts have been made to sanitise it, supposing that the main prayer against the persecutors (vv. 6–19) is a quotation by the psalmist of the persecutor's prayer against him, which is then summed up in the 'thus' of verse 20. However, this really is not justified by the wording and, in any case, does not succeed in its objective, for the psalmist, instead of exercising a nice Christian forgiveness, calls down the same curse on his tormentor!

It is better to accept that this is a really comprehensive, systematic and finely constructed curse. The enemy is to be condemned and his plea for mercy is to make matters worse. He is to lose his livelihood and life itself. His family, now a widow and orphans, is to be torn apart and his property sequestered, his very name blotted out from the records. Not content with the condemnation of the enemy and his children, the curse spreads back up the line to his father and mother, so that their names too are blotted out and only their sin remembered. In a world into which the belief in eternal life had not yet penetrated, the continuance of the family name was all-important; yet this too is to be eradicated, and only a negative memory, the sin of the parents, is to remain. Cursing is to be not merely like clothing stuck to his body, but is to penetrate deep within him.

Standards of politeness, criticism, political correctness and vituperation vary from age to age. The fierce denunciations of John Chrysostom ('John the Silver-mouthed') against the Jews, or Thomas More against Protestants, make uncomfortable and unacceptable reading by today's standards. Even the gentle and shrinking prophet Jeremiah can be roused to ferocity against his tormentors: 'Hand their sons over to famine… Let their wives become childless and widowed. Let their husbands die of plague, their young men be cut down by the sword' (Jeremiah 18:21).

Perhaps it is better to luxuriate in the artistry of the curse and to remember that Old Testament morality merely limited vengeance to the measure of the original offence: 'an eye for an eye and a tooth for a tooth'. The total exclusion of all revenge comes only with the command of Jesus to forgive 70 times seven times. Fully half of Matthew 18, on the community, is occupied with the teaching on forgiveness, and forgiveness is the one petition of the Lord's Prayer that is repeated for emphasis immediately after the prayer. Let the one who is without fault cast the first stone (see John 8:7).

Psalm 109[110]: The Lord's revelation to my Lord

For Christians, this psalm is unique. It is the psalm most often quoted in the New Testament, for it is seen as a direct prophecy of the kingly and priestly rule of the Davidic Messiah, seated at the right hand of the Lord. It makes use of the coronation ritual of the priest-king of Jebusite Jerusalem, who appears in Melchizedek (whose name means 'my king is justice') in Genesis 14, and again in another king of Jerusalem, Adonizedek ('my lord is justice', Joshua 10). This same ritual hymn must have been taken over by David when he captured Jerusalem and made it his capital. The psalm is articulated on the two solemn promises of the Lord to the king. The first three verses celebrate the king's rule, and the next four his priesthood, both conferred by God's irrevocable oath. The Hebrew text, particularly of verse 3, is thoroughly corrupt and therefore impossible to translate with any certainty; but, however it is read, it celebrates the eternal divine origin and destiny of the king.

The promise that the king will be seated at the right hand of God is quoted in Peter's speech at Pentecost to prove the resurrection and exaltation of Christ (Acts 2:34), and again by the writer to the Hebrews to illustrate the eternal and overwhelming rule of Christ (Hebrews 1:13). There is a reference to it also in Jesus' reply to the high priest at the Jewish Sanhedrin hearing, when he declares that he is Messiah, Son of God and Son of Man, sharing God's throne and coming on the clouds of heaven (Mark 14:62). This is the moment in the gospel when his identity is at last revealed. Finally it lies behind the great concluding scene of the book of Revelation, in the new Jerusalem, centred on God and the Lamb, when all creatures venerate him (not them) on *his* throne – a single divinity.

The second promise is the basis of the theology (especially in the letter to the Hebrews) of Christ's priesthood – a new priesthood, no longer the passing priesthood of the Old Testament but the eternal priesthood of Melchizedek, who has no beginning and no end. The risen and glorified Christ, the Lamb standing as though slain, presents his sacrifice once and for all time to the Father for the reconciliation of the human race.

The rather puzzling final verse is again a reference to the Jerusalem priest-king. When David's two sons, Solomon and Adonijah, were struggling for the succession to their dying father's throne, the determining factor seems to have been to draw living water from the only spring of Jerusalem, the spring of Gihon, which lies beside the road at the base of Jerusalem. It is this water that confers legitimacy on the new king (see 1 Kings 1:33, 45).

Psalm 110[111]: I will praise the Lord with all my heart

This is the first of a series of two acrostic psalms, the initial letter of each line working through the Hebrew alphabet from beginning to end. This form seems to have been favoured in the post-exilic era, and the attachment of 'fear of the Lord' to Wisdom also suggests a late date.

It is a psalm of praise, beginning and ending with the thought of praising the Lord. In between, the subjects chosen may be dictated as much by the strict acrostic formula as by any other logic. The psalmist's thought seems to circle round the formative period of the Israelites in the desert of the exodus, when God ransomed them from slavery (v. 9), gave them manna for food (v. 5), formed the covenant with them (vv. 5, 9), and eventually displaced foreign nations for them (v. 6). More striking than this, however, is the constancy of God's care for his people: the word 'forever' occurs in verses 3, 5, 8, 9 and 10. God's unflagging care is seen less in the particular elements mentioned – his works, his righteousness, his strength and his mercy – than in the whole structure of life. Although the historical context of the psalmist's thought is the exodus, the covenant made at that time in the desert continues 'forever' to be the basis of Israel's life. There is a timelessness about the Torah, for it means not only the Book of the Law but, more widely, all the teaching about God and God's ways with the world. The mention of 'wisdom' in the final verse underlines this thought, for the fear of the Lord is the beginning of the covenant and the Torah, no less than of wisdom. 'To fear the Lord is the beginning of wisdom' is simply a more modern way of putting the matter.

The stability and comprehensiveness of the acrostic form, running from *aleph* to *tau*, or from A to Z, gives the psalm an inclusive and satisfying quality. It is a general psalm of praise and thanksgiving, about nothing in particular and yet about all God's dealings with his people. For the Christian, however, the concluding mention of wisdom must bring it to a climax, through the Pauline teaching that Christ himself is the power and the wisdom of God (1 Corinthians 1:24), not to mention the rather quirky insistence that Christ was the rock that followed the Israelites in the desert of the exodus and gave them water (1 Corinthians 10:4). It was Christ who accompanied them as that rabble of runaway slaves was being formed by their experiences into the people of God.

Psalm 111[112]: Blessed the man who fears the Lord

This is the psalm for the successful businessman! There is no getting away from the materialist emphasis of the Old Testament: prosperity is a blessing from the Lord. Abraham was blessed with such increase of flocks and herds that he and his nephew Lot were compelled to split up to find enough grazing. After all his trials, Job was blessed with herds to make the mind boggle – 6,000 camels alone. Since healthy eating and gym clubs were still a fad of the future, to be unashamedly fat was a sign of divine favour.

There are, of course, two other essential dimensions to this blessing of success – justice and generosity. Justice is emphasised three times in the psalm, once with the word that really means 'straightforwardness' or 'fair dealing' (*yashar*), once with a more legal term suggesting discernment and fair judgment (*mishpat*) and once with the more comprehensive term (*zedaqah*) that almost means 'holiness'. The second essential element is generosity, mentioned twice in the psalm. There is no more room for close-fistedness than for crooked dealing.

Alongside the insight that wealth is a blessing of the Lord sits the somewhat paradoxical insistence that it is the poor, impoverished and oppressed who are the Lord's favourites. This idea is never absent from the Bible, visible in the earliest stories of desert hospitality (Abraham entertaining the three strangers, and his servant entertained by Rebekah, in Genesis 18 and 24 respectively), and in the care in so many prescriptions of the law itself to protect the weak, immigrants, widows and orphans. It comes to the fore especially with the experience of destitution in the Babylonian exile, when the Lord's favour becomes focused on the poor, the first recipients of salvation: 'Seek the Lord, all you humble of the earth' (Zephaniah 2:3).

In the gospels we see it especially in Luke, where the poor and disadvantaged welcome the Saviour: no wise men bearing gold and costly spices, but empty-handed, threadbare shepherds come to the newborn displaced person, whose parents cannot afford the full sacrifice in the temple. Warnings of the danger of wealth culminate in the parable of the rich fool who builds himself new barns but has no time to enjoy his wealth (Luke 12:16–21), and a contrast is shown in the story of the centurion whose generosity wins him the cure of his servant (7:1–10). The psalm reminds us that there is no shame in success, but that it does bring its grave responsibilities.

Psalm 112[113]: To the childless wife he gives a home

This psalm begins 'Hallel' or 'Praise!' It opens the group of psalms known as 'the Egyptian Hallel' from its concentration on the deliverance from Egypt (not especially evident in this first psalm). Psalms 112—113[113—114] were sung at the beginning of the Passover Seder, with the first cup of wine.

The psalm has three clear stanzas. The first is an enthusiastic exhortation to praise God, four times repeating the invitation, with an additional 'May the name of the Lord be blessed'. The second and third stanzas, in classic style, give the reasons for praise. The first of these two is praise of the Lord, exalted in the heavens and having complete control of the world from the sweeping dome of the heavens. Only at the end of the stanza comes the specific reason for this concentration on the heavens: God's height in the vast heavens brings out the contrast with his descent to the depths to lift up the lowliest of the lowly.

So we have the same theme – the Lord's care for the disadvantaged and those who humbly trust in him – as we saw in the previous psalm. The focus this time is on the childless, who in some cultures are considered the most deprived of all people. In Africa, celibate clergy and those in religious orders, no matter how comfortably placed they are in material terms, are considered by their childlessness to have given up everything worthwhile. The same has always been true in Judaism, where man and woman were explicitly told to increase and multiply as a part of human nature as it was created by God (Genesis 1:28). In these circumstances, celibacy (where it is maintained) is a strong witness to the overwhelming value of the kingdom of God.

Thus it is apt that the final verse of the psalm repeats the core verse of the thanksgiving song of the supposedly barren Hannah, when she has at last given birth to her son, Samuel (1 Samuel 2:5). In the

Bible there is a whole series of women who seemed destined to remain childless, only to be rescued from childlessness by divine intervention, as part of the plan of salvation history and evidence of God's greater plan: Abraham's wife Sarah, Samson's mother, Elizabeth the mother of John the Baptist. This last verse is echoed also in Mary's Magnificat.

Psalm 113A[114]: When Israel came forth from Egypt

This psalm is an excited, playful and dramatic presentation of the basic story of the creation of Israel as God's people. We do not know exactly what happened at the exodus, for the story was told and retold in the Bible with the continual poetic exaggeration of folk-history, reaching its highest point in this playful psalm. The nearest approach to sober history may be Miriam's ancient triumph-song in Exodus 15: 'Horse and rider he has thrown into the sea...'. There must have been some dramatic escape from pursuing Egyptian forces in which Moses and his straggle of runaway slaves were allowed to get across one of the lakes near what is now the Suez Canal, after which the pursuing forces were blocked. The 'walls of water' of later poetry need no more be taken literally than the Jordan actually turning back on its course (vv. 3, 5). The important factor was that the Lord rescued Israel from overwhelmingly powerful forces. Whatever the basic event, it was seen as the intervention of the strong right arm of the Lord, the introduction to his claiming the people as his own possession.

The continuance of this claim was always described in terms of thunder, lightning and earthquake on Sinai – the mysterious encounter of the covenant, by which God took Israel as his very own, establishing the law of life by which God's people should live. This is expressed in the second verse of our psalm in a way that no decent translation could express. Judah became 'his holy thing', Israel 'his own possession', as though God hugged them to himself like a precious treasure in which no other might share. Henceforth Israel was not like other nations but was dedicated to the Lord, sharing in the Lord's own awesome holiness.

There is a continual pairing of similar images throughout the psalm: Egypt/foreign people, Judah/Israel, sea/Jordan, mountains/hills, rock/flint and pool/spring. What brings delight to the psalm is the playful dramatic personification of the elements: the watery elements of sea and Jordan think better of their natural courses and cannily flee in terror; the solid elements of mountains and hills dance a jig like skittish lambs. These pictures come more easily in a culture where ideas of river-spirits and mountain-gods were familiar.

The numbering of the Psalms goes into freefall here, for the Greek version (the version of the Bible which, for the first 400 years of the Christian Church, was considered the only authentic text) joins into one psalm the Hebrew 114 and 115, despite the obvious differences between them. The reverse process occurs in Hebrew 116, which the Greek divides into two, meaning that the Greek ends up still one behind.

Psalm 113B[115]: Not to us, O Lord, but to your name

The clue to this whole psalm lies in the first four verses, a contrast between the God of Israel and the man-made idols of the nations. These idols are very prominent in the thought of the psalmist, in a way reminiscent of the second part of Isaiah (chapters 40—56). This part of Isaiah was written in Babylon during the exile, when Israel was brought face to face with a flourishing cult of idols.

Till then, Israel had been content to proclaim the Lord as its God without concerning itself with other nations and their own protector-gods. It was generally assumed in the Near East that gods were territorial. As already mentioned, this was why Naaman, the Syrian general cured of leprosy by Elisha, assumed that the Lord could be worshipped only on the soil of Israel, and accordingly took home to Damascus two donkey-loads of the soil to stand on while he prayed (2 Kings 5:17). (In the same way, that good Yorkshirewoman St Helena, mother of the Emperor Constantine, took shiploads of soil from Jerusalem on which to build her church, Santa Croce in Gerusalemme, in Rome.) However, for Israel, the Babylonian exile was a great turning point and deepening point in their understanding of God. Confronted with the multiple and varied idols of Babylon, the author of Isaiah 40—56 pours out several satirical set-pieces, mocking the folly of worshipping carved idols. Such weird attempts to depict gods must have seemed even weirder to a people for whom all graven images were banned as a blasphemous limitation of the God who was totally other. Our western culture and religion are so inured to classical, Renaissance and even Christian statuary that we can have little notion of the shock and horror that would have been occasioned by such attempts to pull the deity down to a humanly intelligible level. God is not meant to be understood, only worshipped. God is not meant to be comfortable, only awesome.

The exiles could only pray that some semblance of due glory might be given to the name, to the power enshrined in the unpronounceable name, for 'our God, the maker of heaven and earth, does whatever he wills' (v. 3). 'To your name give the glory' means the same as the first two petitions of the prayer Jesus taught his disciples: 'May your name be held holy, may your kingship come' (Luke 11:2). God's kingship can be fully recognised only when the gentle and loving power of his name is acknowledged by all the living and the dead. It was this that Jesus came to foster and demonstrate by his miracles and his teaching, and, finally, by the loving obedience of his death.

Psalm 114—115[116]: I love the Lord, for he has heard my cry

Death, or rather deliverance from death, is written all over this psalm. The psalmist praises God for rescuing him from the snares of death, the anguish of Sheol (v. 3), in a way that seems to be more than just poetic imagery. The whole poem is a song of praise for rescue, expressed most strongly by raising the cup of salvation and making a thanksgiving sacrifice. Yet, in verse 15, in the second half of the psalm (unless the Greek translation was correct in splitting the psalm in two), he acknowledges that in the eyes of the Lord, the death of his faithful is precious. Does this mean that the Lord welcomes the death of his faithful? Or that the death of his faithful costs the Lord dear? Or, thirdly, that such a death is of major significance to the Lord? It is difficult to know, and none of these interpretations is wholly satisfactory.

Two other factors must bear on the interpretation of the psalm and its view of death. Firstly, belief in any sort of life with the Lord after death became explicit in Israel only in the second century before Christ, at the time of the Maccabean persecution. Nevertheless, there had existed long before then, at least since the time of the book of Job, a firm belief that the Lord's love for his chosen ones would never lapse or desert them: 'I know that my Redeemer lives... then in my flesh I shall see God' (Job 19:25-26, NRSV). The implications of this belief had not yet become explicit, although Psalm 72[73] can say, 'You were holding me by my right hand... and then you will lead me to glory' (vv. 23-24).

A second factor which may be borne in mind is that in 2 Corinthians 4:13-14 Paul quotes verse 10 (according to the Greek division, the first verse of Psalm 115) as the grounds of his hope and persever-ance in the persecutions and worries of the apostolate: 'we, too, *believe* and therefore we, too, *speak*, realising that he who raised up the Lord Jesus will raise us up with Jesus in our turn'. Whatever its meaning in our own analysis, for Paul this psalm was an assurance of his hope in resurrection and life with Christ. We can afford to make this hope our own.

Psalm 116[117]: O praise the Lord, all you nations

Is this little psalm worth commenting on, or can it simply be brushed under the carpet? It's definitely worth some comment! It gives the lie to any conception of a self-satisfied Israel, which thought of itself as the chosen people to the exclusion of all others. It also creates a puzzle for Christians.

From the first call of Abraham, as we have it now in Genesis 12:1–3, the choice of Abraham as a great nation implicated all peoples, who would 'bless themselves by him'. The choice cannot be seen as exclusive. Of course, the implications of this phrase took time to be fully understood, and it was not until the period of the Babylonian exile and beyond that Israel became sufficiently conscious of other nations to concern itself about their salvation. From then onwards, and already in the later chapters of Isaiah and in the later prophets, it becomes a standard feature that all nations will come to draw salvation from Jerusalem: 'all the nations will stream to' the temple in Jerusalem (Isaiah 2:2). Jesus, having no form of transport other than his own two feet, had little contact with Gentiles, but challenged and then responded to the faith of the Syro-Phoenician who sought healing for her daughter, and crossed into the Gentile Decapolis to heal the Gerasene demoniac. This proved sufficient warrant for Peter and then Paul to extend the mission of the church into the Gentile world.

But how are all nations brought to praise the Lord? How can we say that all those who are saved are saved by Christ? Even if they have never even heard of Christ? Is 'No salvation outside the church' a medieval European doctrine, exploded by the discovery of a world beyond Europe? Vatican II envisaged a series of concentric circles. The inner circle is those Christians in union with the Bishop of Rome; then there are wider bands of others who see their salvation in Christ, still others who acknowledge God under names such as Yahweh or Allah, and finally believers who seek God under other signs and symbols. What of the other world religions? The globalisation of the 21st century has brought us to realise the value of the great religions of the east and their positive function in promoting the commitment and qualities treasured by Christians. Can we say of such believers that, even though they have no historical link with Jesus Christ, nevertheless he is the mediator of their salvation? Are they, too, 'latent' or 'anonymous' Christians?

Psalm 117[118]: Go forward in procession with branches

This festive psalm of celebration is clearly a processional chant. It begins and ends with a bracket of praise to the Lord 'for he is good' (vv. 1, 29) and centres on 'The Lord is my strength' (v. 14). The first half has many features of a triumph-song – for example, the introductory refrain, 'his mercy endures forever', four times stated; the appeal for help and the exaggerated claims of bloody victory (vv. 10–12), which are so typical of Near Eastern victory inscriptions of the time. The second half of the psalm develops the processional idea, as the cortège enters the temple.

Later rabbinic sources speak of this psalm as being used for the festival of Sukkoth or Tabernacles, which fits well with the mention of a procession with branches (v. 27), for this was, and is, the festival when Jews build and live in temporary shelters made of branches. These shelters commemorate the temporary homes of the Israelites during their 40 years of travelling through the desert of Sinai – a reminder that there is no abiding city on this earth.

In the New Testament context, this psalm brings us to Palm Sunday, both because of the branches and because of verse 26, 'Blest is he who comes in the name of the Lord', which was sung at Jesus' messianic entry into Jerusalem (Mark 11:9). Mark never worries about sequential chronology, and it is tempting to suggest that he took this scene from the approach to Sukkoth (which occurs in the autumn) and used it to illustrate Jesus' climactic entry on his final visit to Jerusalem. How aware were they, at the time, of the significance of this scene? Were Jesus and his disciples simply caught up in the celebrations of the festival, entering with the crowds of other pilgrims, but in such a way that the event later took on a messianic significance? Perhaps only later did they realise that the branches and the chant were directed to Jesus, as bringing the kingship of God to a new reality. John grants that the significance of Jesus' replacement of the temple building with the temple of his body (John 2:21) was appreciated only after his resurrection. The gospel accounts frequently show us the events of Jesus' life in the glow of inspired later understanding, imparted after Pentecost by reflection in the Spirit (see John 7:39). Further reminiscence occurs in Jesus' reference to himself as the stone rejected by the builders, which has become the cornerstone (v. 22; see Mark 12:10).

Psalm 118[119]: Blessed are those whose way is blameless

Who would sing a love song about law? Yet this is just what the present psalm is! In Israel, the Law is a precious gift, a love-present from the Lord. In our modern conception of law, the law is considered as restrictive, compelling, something to be pushed to the limit, but for the Israelite it is liberating and a delight. The Law is the ideal present from the Lord. Obedience to the Law is not a tiresome obligation but a loving response to a loving gift, enabling the Israelite to approach God in loving humility and gratitude.

An ideal present continues to remind us of the giver, for it is chosen with attention, care and personal consideration, as a real mark of love between friends. Just so, the Law is God's charter of friendship, showing the Israelites what they must do and be if they are to be God's people. Thereby it shows the nature of God, for my presents show my own nature, what I value in my friend, and one of our most intimate means of communication with each other. Quite apart from the general nature of gift-giving, this becomes especially clear in the case of the Law, for so many of the precepts of the Law are framed by the imitation of God: 'Be holy as I am holy'; 'Remember the widow, the orphan and the immigrant among you, as I remembered you when you were widows, orphans and immigrants in Egypt.' Humankind is made in the image of God, male and female, but needs God's guidance to fulfil that image, and this is what the Law provides.

Notionally the Law was given by or, at least, through Moses (the paradigm case being the Ten Commandments written 'by the finger of God') but in fact it was the product of a series of decisions in particular instances of case-law over several centuries. Many of the decisions were in conformity with the case-law of surrounding peoples, but, in the case of the people of God, we would regard their adoption as being guided by the Holy Spirit. Two of the profound motivations behind them are the safeguarding of the holiness of God and the safeguarding of respect for every individual.

Such is the meaning of the affectionate and often even rapturous terms used of the Law in this long poem. As a poem, too, it is a *tour de force*. It falls into sections of eight verses, every verse in each section beginning with the same letter of the alphabet, and working successively through the alphabet. We have met this form of acrostic before – for example, in Psalms 24[25] and 33[34] – but in these cases only for single verses, not groups of eight verses. The terms used for the provisions of the Law are also remarkably varied, though it is difficult to weigh the precise differences between them.

Psalm 119[120]: Friction in the tents of Qedar

Here begin the 15 Psalms of Ascent, each of which has the heading 'Song of Goings Up'. What precisely this means is unknown. A fairly late Jewish tradition associates these psalms with 15 steps leading up to the inner sanctuary of the temple; this may or may not be pure invention. They all make clear, however, that there was something special about going up to Jerusalem. One may well imagine that they were songs of joy sung by groups of pilgrims on their way up to Jerusalem for the major feasts, meeting up with other groups of pilgrims in greater and greater throngs, all coming from the strains and difficulties of living out their faith in unbelieving Gentile lands. Still today there are educated Jews who think that Jerusalem is the centre of the world in a quasi-territorial way. The spirit of these psalms is the enduring help of the Lord, beamed from Jerusalem and becoming ever more reassuring and comforting as its source is approached. For Christians, too, these Psalms of Ascents are the perfect expression of the theology of pilgrimage so richly expressed in Hebrews 4: we are a pilgrim people, still on our way to the ultimate sanctuary of the Lord.

A clear feature of this psalm is the two place names in verse 5. They already betoken a meeting of pilgrims from faraway places, for Qedar seems to be located in northern Arabia, a symbol of distant desolation (Isaiah 42:11; Jeremiah 49:28–29), and Meshech considerably further north, in the area of the Caucasus. The two of them may be considered to stand for outlandish distant places. The other feature that the psalmist is glad to escape is labelled as deception and lying (v. 2). Were the two places inhabited only by compulsive liars? Rather than referring to persistent attempts to deceive the psalmist personally, he is more likely to be characterising idolatrous worship as deceit. This is seen in the prophets as a deliberate refusal to acknowledge the truth that Yahweh is Lord of the world and all things (see, for example, Hosea 12:1; Jeremiah 9:4). In this case, the believer rejoices to get away from a twisted, distorted and so deceptive worldview. Disagreement over the ultimate truths of God and religion would also provide a better background for the friction described in the last verse of the psalm, the psalmist's longing for peace and the constant rebuttal with hostility.

Psalm 120[121]: I lift up my eyes to the mountains

Holy mountains play a part in many religious rituals, fuelled by the inaccessibility, solitude, danger and inherent nobility of mountains. It is not just that the mountains are thought to be nearer heaven (as in the attempt to reach heaven by means of the tower of Babel), but that they remain mysterious and remote, unshakeable as the swirl of storm and thunder sweeps over them. Mount Olympus was the home of the gods in Greece, and the snow on Mount Kilimanjaro was held to be the sitting-cushion of the gods. The Hebrew–Christian tradition is no exception: the psalmist lifts up his eyes to the mountains, from where shall come his hope. (Grammatically, the second line of verse 1 could be understood as a question, but this would leave the first line oddly inconsequential.)

In Hebrew thought, the holy mountain *par excellence* is Mount Sinai. Tradition places this at Gebel Musa ('the mountain of Moses'), which is indeed an awesome mountain. In the burning heat of the Sinai desert, there is no earth to mitigate the severity, only rock and the sand produced by the silent friction of the winds. By midday even the camels are panting. The drama of the place is increased by the sombre shades of rock, some grey granite, others a rusty iron-ore hue, others again almost a sulphurous green, but all noble, as they soar in shards towards the sky. This is the traditional place where Israel underwent its formative experience of the Lord as its protector-God. Here also (but under the alternative name of Mount Horeb) the prophet Elijah met God in the 'voice of silence' and veiled his head in reverence (1 Kings 19:12–13).

In the New Testament, Moses and Elijah join Jesus on the holy mountain of the transfiguration, where the chosen three disciples experience his divinity before the passion. As the new Moses, Jesus in Matthew's gospel gives his new law on the holy mountain in the form of the Sermon on the Mount (chs. 5—7), just as Moses had given the Law on Sinai. Finally, as the awesome Son of Man, who has received 'all power in heaven and on earth' from the Ancient One (Daniel 7:13; Matthew 28:16–20), the risen Christ sends out his disciples from the holy mountain to teach all nations.

In Psalm 120[121], God is unsleeping (v. 4) – like the mountain, which is there as a guard, ever alert and unchanging. It provides shade from the sun by day and, eerily, from the moon by night. Majestic and unconquered, it guards our going and coming. The mountain is indeed a noble symbol of the protective power of God.

Psalm 121[122]: Pray for the peace of Jerusalem

In two short verses, the psalmist envisages both the beginning of the pilgrimage, when he was invited to join the journey, and its end, standing within the gates of Jerusalem. This evokes diverse kinds of memories for me: for instance, the joy and excitement in an El Al plane when the signs for landing are switched on and the Hebrew song spreads swiftly through the passenger area: 'How good and pleasant it is, brothers seated together' (Psalm 132[133]:1). Or a memory from the time when Jerusalem was still an international city – the sight of bent old men, lifetime pilgrims to Mecca, making the long and arduous journey in cattle-trucks, staggering their way into the second-holiest shrine of Islam, the Dome of the Rock. Or the view from Castel, the fortified hilltop, a day's march to the west of Jerusalem, from where the Crusaders, coming up from the coast, first caught sight of their goal on the skyline. 'It is there that the tribes go up, the tribes of the Lord.'

The etymology here given to the name is 'City of Peace', based on the word for 'peace', *shalom*, but a strong contender is 'City (or Foundation) of Salem', a Semitic god. The Hebrew of verse 6 gives a lovely medley of sounds based on *shalom*: *sha'alu shalom yerushalayim yishlehu ohavayik*, literally 'Ask peace for Jerusalem; they shall be at ease, those who love her.' The prayer for peace is appropriate, for Jerusalem is, sadly, a city of strife and tension. Well known is the long-standing strife between Jews and Muslims (or between Israelis and Palestinians) regularly fuelled by reprisals of various kinds by either side and total unwillingness to compromise. Only slightly less public is the constant hassle between different branches of Christianity, where the Holy Sepulchre itself is riven by strife between the three owners (Latin, Greek and Armenian) to the extent that the 'armistice' imposed by the Ottoman Empire two centuries ago still prescribes the allotment of times and places. This 'armistice' is administered by Muslims. Every hierarchical tradition of Christianity seems to have its own Patriarch – Catholic, Orthodox, Syrian, Latin, Greek, Armenian, Coptic, Ethiopic. Only Lutherans and Anglicans stand slightly aside, with a bishop 'in' Jerusalem rather than 'of' Jerusalem. Prayer for peace is sorely needed, for nowhere in the world is the scandal of Christian disunity, the failure of Christians to achieve the unity for which Christ prayed at the last supper, so obvious and so painful.

Psalm 122[123]: To you have I lifted up my eyes

The chief metaphor in this psalm is striking – the close attention of the eastern servant or slave to the whim of his or her master, utterly attentive to the least indication of eyebrow or gesture. To recognise a slight movement may be a matter of life or death. Such, maintains the psalmist, is his attention to the will of the Lord. The first feature, then, is the utter dependence of humanity on God. We have no grounds for any comeback or protest to God: we can only accept what we are given.

The other striking feature is that this metaphor is expressed in female as well as male terms: the eyes of a slave-girl are fixed on the gestures of her mistress, just as the eyes of the male slave are on the gestures of his master. As we will soon see, with regard to Psalm 130[131], there is no sexual discrimination in God: men and women are treated alike, and God has neither male nor female characteristics to the exclusion of female or male features. God may, or must, be conceived in female terms no less than male, with feminine sensitivity as well as masculine strength, with acceptance no less than assertiveness.

In this poem, the longing for Zion comes into view in the longing to be free of the scorn and contempt of the arrogant. This may well be focusing on the contempt and unpopularity experienced by diaspora Jews among the Gentiles for their fidelity to the Lord. Both Gentile and Jewish sources attest the mockery undergone by Jews for their fidelity to their faith in the ancient as in the modern world. Faith always runs the risk of being mocked as credulity and gullibility. Religious practices always run the risk of appearing – and, indeed, of being – hypocritical. It has always been part of the vocation of the people of God, as the servant of the Lord, bearing witness to divine values, to be liable to mockery by those who do not share those values.

In the Greek version of the psalm, the poet twice in verse 3 uses the same words as would later be used by the Canaanite woman who sought healing for her daughter from Jesus, and would also become standard in the liturgy: *Kyrie eleison*, 'Lord, have mercy'. Just so, we put ourselves unreservedly in the hands of God.

Psalm 123[124]: The snare of the fowler

Two striking images of threat dominate this psalm – the rushing water and the snare of the fowler. The Israelites were always afraid of the sea, not only because of its uncontrollable force but also because of the powerful creation story that we have already encountered, in which God divided the waters to insert the world. The waters still surround the world, and God is still holding back the waters from engulfing it. If he ceased to do so, the mighty flood would engulf the world. More practically frightening is the flood of water in a dry wadi. Within hours of the winter rains, the tidal wave of a flashflood, several metres high, can suddenly sweep down the dry bed of an enclosed canyon in the desert with inescapable force and the fury of 'raging waters'. The noted French biblical scholar Jean Steinmann was drowned with a score of other visitors to Petra by just such a flood in 1963.

I once saw a fowler's snare in operation on a patch of waste ground in Jerusalem. The fowler lays out on the ground a net some metres square, with hinged wings of similar netting. When the small birds are fluttering and squabbling over the bait placed in the middle of the net, the wings of netting are silently raised by means of strings and fall on the birds, trapping them inescapably. The psalmist prays to be delivered from just such a trap.

The dangers of a journey to Jerusalem would have been considerable. We may compare Paul's summary of risks confronting a traveller: 'I have been in danger from rivers, in danger from brigands, in danger from my own people and in danger from the Gentiles, in danger in the towns and in danger in the open country, in danger at sea and in danger from people masquerading as brothers' (2 Corinthians 11:26). On the roads and in the open countryside there was little rule of law, and kidnapping for the lucrative business of slavery was particularly rife during the final centuries before Christ. Those who could afford it would travel with an armed guard; those who could not might well be left without the succour of any good Samaritan 'when people rose against' them. They would be conscious of the need for divine protection especially at the beginning of the pilgrimage, decreasing as the throngs of pilgrims thickened and they could relax with thankfulness.

Psalm 124[125]: Those who put their trust in the Lord

The original Jebusite city of Jerusalem, which David captured and made his capital, is indeed low-lying and nestles within a protective circle of hills. It is a low point on the spine of the country that runs north–south, and a crossing-point on the east–west road that runs from the coast to the great trade routes of the east. Before Solomon joined it to the hill to its north by his massive infill, the city was sufficiently isolated to form a defensive citadel but could never realistically claim to be higher than the other mountains. By a stroke of genius, David captured this strong but small city, lying between the northern territories (Saul's kingdom) and his own southern sphere of influence (Judah), and made it his capital, uniting the two territories around his own personal fiefdom. By an even greater stroke of genius, he installed the ark of the covenant there and, by so doing, made it also the Lord's capital, although he himself did not succeed in building the temple which was to make it the holy city of all holy cities. There was a certain air of patronage in his offer to build the Lord a house – an offer that the Lord refused, replying with the even more significant promise to build David a house (a dynasty) that would endure forever.

As a holy city, Jerusalem's name is Zion. The Lord is enthroned in Zion, as several of the psalms relate. It is from Zion that the Lord will rule over all peoples. 'Zion' is Isaiah's preferred name for Jerusalem as the throne of the 'Holy One of Israel', which is Isaiah's favourite title for God. In the New Testament also, it is to Zion that the Messiah comes, riding on a donkey (Matthew 21:5, quoting Zechariah 9:9), and Mount Zion is the heavenly Jerusalem 'where the millions of angels have gathered for the festival' (Hebrews 12:22) and where the Lamb will take his stand with all those who are saved (Revelation 14:1).

At the end of time, Zion will be raised up by divine favour to dominate the surrounding hills, as a sign of divine exaltation rather than natural contours, a matter of eschatology rather than geography. Meanwhile, the circle of hills protecting Zion is a firm image of the Lord's sure protection for his holy and faithful people, those who put their trust in the Lord. The psalm is a splendid expression of the joy of God's people returning from living among unbelievers to their Lord's own home.

Psalm 125[126]: We thought we were dreaming

The positioning of this psalm among the pilgrimage psalms, the Songs of Ascent, gives it a special tone. It seems to fall into two halves, the first hopeful, the second more realistic.

The first half is full of joy and carefree laughter at the people's release from captivity in Babylon. In 539BC, King Cyrus of Persia won Babylon in what he claimed to be a bloodless victory. Within two years he had sent home captives from all the subject peoples who had been detained in Babylon. For the Jews who had spent a notional 70 years in captivity, this must have been a moment of delirious joy, as suggested in the first half of the psalm. It seemed like a dream come true – like streams in the Negeb, the daunting dry desert to the south of Israel. Perhaps the psalmist is referring to the short-lived torrents that flow for a few hours after the heavy winter rains, which seem miraculous. Or perhaps he means a total transformation of the thirsty desert into well-watered countryside, which would be a real, inconceivable miracle – the hand of God fostering his people.

With verse 4, however, a more sober realism sets in – a prayer for the complete ending of the exile. A century before the transportation of the Judeans to Babylon, the ten tribes of the northern kingdom of Israel had been deported to somewhere in the Assyrian empire, to be dispersed and never seen again; Israel would not be complete until they were gathered in as well. Even after Cyrus' decree of release, many Jews remained in Babylon or scattered in small communities of the diaspora around the eastern Mediterranean. It was from these places that we can presume the pilgrims were gathering as they sang on the way to Jerusalem. The exile would not be truly over until they too had been reunited into a single people.

For Christians, as the pilgrim people of God, this ingathering is the eschatological gathering depicted by Paul, when, at the trumpet-call of the angel, Christ's followers will join him in a triumphal procession in the clouds (1 Thessalonians 4:16). It is spoken of with longing in Hebrews 4:1–11 as the goal of the pilgrimage to the promised 'place of rest', which was never reached during the 40 years of wandering in the desert.

Psalm 126[127]: If the Lord does not build the house

Two features of this attractive little prayer make it unique among the Psalms of Ascent. It is the only one that has no mention of Jerusalem or going up to Jerusalem on pilgrimage. It is more a Wisdom psalm, a reflection on the Wisdom truth that all success comes from the Lord. This is illustrated through the two meanings of 'house': a house of bricks and mortar, and a house in the sense of family or dynasty. Why was it included among these psalms? Presumably because of the idea of building a city, for the city of Jerusalem is still the goal of pilgrimage, and building up and guarding the city in every way is always important in the Psalms of Ascent.

The other unique feature is the dedication to Solomon, given in the title. This is, no doubt, the result of the words 'he pours gifts on his beloved' (v. 2), with its use of the endearing pet-name 'beloved of Yahweh, the Lord', *Yedid-Yah*, given to Solomon by the prophet Nathan (2 Samuel 12:25). 'His beloved' is assumed to be Solomon in this case also.

The first application of the Wisdom reflection offers one side of a theology of work: no matter how hard, how early and how late we toil, without the Lord's blessing all the effort is in vain. The Hebrew word used for 'in vain' is *shav*, a word so light and insubstantial that it almost flies out of the window by itself. The prophet Jeremiah loves to use it (see, for example, 2:30; 4:30) to denote the ineffectiveness of human efforts unblessed by God – a mere puff of wind.

The second application takes us to a scene of negotiation at the city gate (v. 5). This was where the elders gathered, where business was transacted before an appropriate crowd of onlookers who would act as witnesses, as when Abraham negotiated with the elders of Hebron for a burial-plot of land (Genesis 23), or when Boaz negotiated for the hand of Ruth in marriage (Ruth 4). Not only are children, the 'fruit of the womb', the delight of a mother (v. 3), but the man who has a clutch of beefy sons at his back is more likely to succeed in such business deals!

It is attractive to think that the phrase 'when he pours gifts on his beloved while they slumber' (v. 2) is echoed in the gospel parable of the seed growing secretly, which grows 'while he sleeps, when he is awake… how, he does not know' (Mark 4:27).

Psalm 127[128]: Your wife like a fruitful vine

This psalm must have been attracted to its present position by the blessing on the fruit of the womb at the end of the previous psalm. The beatitude formula ('Blessed are…') marks it out as a Wisdom psalm, teaching about where the Lord's blessing falls. Again, it is not work in itself that brings a reward, for this must be accompanied and inspired by reverence or fear of the Lord.

The psalm is reassuringly even-handed, with a blessing first on the labouring man, then on the mother of the family, and finally on the family itself. Then, as now, the family is an important factor in Judaism. At the very end comes the blessing of peace on the whole nation of Israel.

The blessing is expressed from the husband's point of view, but the images of the fruitful vine and the young shoots of the olive have a feminine tenderness. It is often said that the Bible is unacceptably male-dominated. This accusation is not altogether without foundation, for some of the authors (for example, Ben Sira in the Apocrypha) seem to regard women as simply fickle and a snare to weak males. More worrying is some of the imagery, for infidelity to the Lord is often associated with female prostitution and adultery, without any cognisance of the fact that men can be at least as unfaithful as women. On the other side, God's love for humanity is represented not merely in the neutral imagery of a parent's love (Hosea 11:1–4) but also in the imagery of a mother's tenderness (Isaiah 66:12–13) and a mother's gut-love for her children (Isaiah 49:15; Psalm 76[77]:9, using for 'tenderness' a word related to 'womb').

Furthermore, it must be accepted that plenty of strong, courageous, admirable women are depicted in the Bible. It is perhaps not so admirable that it is Eve who leads Adam astray. Later, however, we have the sturdy Rebekah, who drew water for ten camels after their desert journey – perhaps 100 gallons (Genesis 24:20), the warlike Deborah (Judges 5), the self-sacrificing daughter of Jephthah (Judges 11), Ruth, and Judith in the Apocrypha, whose spirit put her menfolk to shame. In the New Testament, quite apart from Mary the mother of Christ, there are powerful apostolic women such as Chloe, Phoebe, Priscilla and Junia. In an era and a culture where women were seldom remarked, this was an important degree of recognition and honour.

Psalm 128[129]: A harvest blessing

This short prayer falls crisply into two halves. The first three verses are an assertion of perseverance through the long series of persecutions that Israel endures, and trust in the protection of the Lord. It is reminiscent of Paul's splendid passage: 'We are in difficulties on all sides, but never cornered; we see no answer to our problems, but never despair; we have been persecuted, but never deserted; knocked down, but never killed; always, wherever we may be, we carry with us in our body the death of Jesus, so that the life of Jesus, too, may always be seen in our body' (2 Corinthians 4:8–10, JB). Paul's passage is further enriched by the Christian idea of sharing sufferings with Christ, through sharing in the life of Christ.

In the second half of the psalm, we encounter (in a fairly mild form) the long-standing problem of prayer against the psalmist's persecutors. The arresting image of the dry grass on the flat roof of a Palestinian house recalls that a Palestinian roof serves to keep out the sun as much as the rain. The long strands of elephant-grass become more and more brittle and yellow over the course of the summer. They are not useless, however; they merely serve a different purpose from the rich corn harvested by the armful later in the season. They are still serving that purpose even if the binder does not gather them joyfully into sheaves! At least we are spared any fierce imprecatory prayers about breaking the teeth of the wicked and annihilating the memory of the psalmist's enemies, which have appeared in other psalms. It suffices, however, as a reminder both that the Christian demand to set aside all revenge still lay in the future, and that this demand goes against all instincts and remains as difficult to fulfil as it ever was.

The joy and good humour of harvest time are nicely evoked by the scattering of blessings in the final couplet. I always remember an occasion when I was walking past a banana-grove in Israel and the owner spontaneously plucked a couple of bananas from the plant and offered me one. As he blessed his own, he said, 'It is such a joy to be able to thank the Lord for the fruits of the earth.'

Psalm 129[130]: De profundis

This psalm has been additionally sanctified by its use in Christian prayer for the dead. It has become almost the primary expression of Christian hope. In fact, the only oblique allusion to death is in the first line, 'the depths', which may mean the abyss of Sheol, the world of the dead, though it need not do so. The phrase can certainly be used more widely, of any extreme distress. In the context of the Songs of Ascent, it is the cry of hope voiced by the pilgrim approaching Jerusalem from the loneliness of the diaspora.

There are three clues that give specific meaning to the psalm and colour to the hope. The first is the image of the watchman, looking out for the dawn (v. 6). No one who has ever had an overnight vigil can be blind to the magical quality of that image, as one looks towards the east, espying – or again and again thinking one espies – the first light of dawn. Then (as Horatio describes it in the first scene of Shakespeare's *Hamlet*), 'the morn, in russet mantle clad, walks o'er the dew of yon high eastward hill'.

The second clue is a series of words of loving and longing. The longing for forgiveness (v. 4) is itself an expression of love, a longing for closeness rather than any self-interest, especially when allied to the other expressions. The Hebrew conveys it with wonderful intensity and succinctness: 'I hope in the Lord, my soul is waiting, I wait upon his word, my soul to the Lord' (vv. 5–6). 'My soul' stands for the psalmist's whole being or whole self; the sense is only weakened by the unavoidable English supplement, 'my soul *belongs/is turned/ is directed* to the Lord'. The reason given is that with the Lord there is *hesed*, so often weakly translated as 'mercy' – a condescending, frightened word for what is really the unfailing family love of a mother or a sibling.

The final thought comes in the double mention of redemption (vv. 7, 8). The Christian thinks of Christ the redeemer, who has bought us from our captivity at the great price of his blood: 'you have been bought at a price' (1 Corinthians 6:20; 7:23). There, the association may be the purchase and setting free of a slave in the Roman world. The Israelite, however, thought of God more as the redeemer from captivity in Egypt or as the liberator from exile in Babylon, for liberation from captivity is the classic association of redemption in the Old Testament.

Psalm 130[131]: God as mother

Like the previous psalm, this one stresses waiting for the Lord. A difference, however, is that this psalm does not ask for anything. There is no element of petition, only a tranquil and unpretentious peace and contentment, compared to the peace of a full-fed baby on its mother – not specifically 'on its mother's breast', as it is sometimes translated. This is a prayer of contentment, not a prayer of petition; it consists of resting in the presence of God as mother.

God is customarily compared to a father, conceived as the originator of life. God is also often pictured as a stern father who is a figure of correction, although the popular conception of the God of the Old Testament as a God of wrath by contrast to the God of love in the New Testament is quite unjustified. However, this image of the full-fed baby, at rest on its mother, is perhaps the warmest instance of God's motherhood. God's love is compared to a mother's love especially in the second part of Isaiah: 'Does a woman forget the baby at her breast, or fail to cherish the son of her womb? Yet even if these forget, I will never forget you' (Isaiah 49:15, JB). The love of God is even more intense than the most intense of all human loves, that of a mother feeding her child. Correspondingly, the trust and contentment that we owe to God are more intense than those of a baby with its mother.

We may ask why this reflection is included in the Psalms of Ascent to Jerusalem. The answer is that Jerusalem is compared to the mother, as also in Psalm 86[87] (a city in every language is depicted in feminine, motherly terms). In Isaiah 66:9–13, Jerusalem is the mother who treats her children with infinite tenderness, while the Lord is in the position of a midwife, bringing to birth and then sending peace, flowing like a river, comforting her children as a son is comforted by his mother.

We cannot restrict the imagery of God's love. In the Song of Songs, God's love for Israel (or the Church) is the questing, teasing, varying love of young lovers. In Hosea 2, God's love is the passionate love of spouses. In Hosea 11, it is the love of parent for child. Perhaps the most frequent mention of God's love is in *hesed*, the love within a family that will never let its members down.

Psalm 131[132]: O Lord, remember David

This is a prayer about David's determination to bring the ark of the covenant up to its due place in Jerusalem. The story of David and the ark is fascinating. In the early period of Israel's history, on the journey through the desert, the ark was held to be the actual dwelling-place of the Lord on earth, protecting and guiding the people. So when, under Eli's leadership, the Israelites went into battle against the steadily encroaching Philistines, they took the ark with them to sustain them and to frighten the enemy. However, their wickedness was such that the Lord was not prepared to win a victory for them, and the ark itself was captured (1 Samuel 4:11). But the Lord showed his displeasure by giving his captors the humiliating disease of piles. Consequently they sent the ark to the borders of their territory, first at Beth-Shemesh and then at Kiriath-Yearim ('the plains of Yearim' in v. 6), where it seems to have lain neglected for some time.

When David captured Jerusalem and made it his personal capital, he further enhanced this master-stroke by bringing the ark to Jerusalem, with great ceremony, from Kiriath-Yearim. Thus he made his capital also the shrine of the Lord upon earth – a politico-religious coup for David (2 Samuel 6). This was the beginning of the mystique of Jerusalem as the earthly icon of God's dwelling-place in heaven. David even offered to build a house for the Lord, only to receive a sharp but loving rejection through his prophet. It is not for any human being to patronise God in this way. Instead, the Lord promised that he would build a house for David, meaning a dynasty. The sovereignty of this house is described in God's promise (one version of which occurs in this psalm, vv. 11–12), expressed in idealised and poetic terms, which we can now see to be fulfilled in a new and eschatological sense in the sovereignty of God and Jesus in the New Testament. So this prayer is a treasure for Christians also.

The occasion of the psalm is not easy to decide. Was it composed for the actual entry of the ark into Jerusalem, or was it used at a repeat celebration of the event, perhaps an annual festivity? It is full of confidence in the dynasty of David and in the established worship of the temple.

Psalm 132[133]: How good and pleasant it is

This psalm is dominated by two comfortable and luxurious images that breathe contentment. The first is the family party, where brothers are gathered together. In the context of the pilgrimage to Zion, this is the coming together of a 'fictive family' (in other words, not a natural blood family, but a family of people who have forged similar bonds together) from the disparate parts of the diaspora on the way to Jerusalem, in an ever-thickening stream as they approach the city. It can be effortlessly applied to the Christian family of brothers – or, indeed, brothers and sisters.

The image of the oil running down the beard refers to the ancient Near Eastern custom (in a world where scarcity of water restricted the possibilities of washing!) of placing a cone of fragrant unguent on the head of each of the diners at a banquet, which would gradually melt in the heat of the evening, spreading its fragrance throughout the room or the tent.

Mount Hermon, at nearly 3,000 metres, is the highest point in Syria and is rich in moisture. Its three peaks are snow-covered for much of the year, with a three-month ski-season. It is, of course, a highly poetic exaggeration to imagine that the dew of Hermon could actually fall on Mount Zion, some 200 kilometres to the south, but the melting snows and the heavy dew of summer provide much of the water that flows into the Jordan, then into the Lake of Galilee, and finally into the Dead Sea. Pilgrims from the north would wonder at Mount Hermon on their left as they began the journey down the great rift valley that runs from north of Damascus down as far as Kenya. No doubt, they would think of the fruitfulness brought by its melting snows and dew into the more southerly parts of the land.

Water is the natural image for life, since it is the source and fuel of all life. The psalm takes this one step further with the words 'there the Lord gives his blessing, life forever'. Judaism used this imagery for the Law as the source of a fuller life. In Ezekiel 47, water flows from the temple, bringing life and fish even to the odiferous and inert Dead Sea. In Christianity we think more of the invitation of Jesus as the source of eternal life in John 7:37–38: 'Let anyone who is thirsty come to me! Let anyone who believes in me come and drink!'

Psalm 133[134]: O come, bless the Lord!

This short and peaceful psalm brings the series of Songs of Ascent to a fitting conclusion. It is full of praise and thanks and blessing, and is clearly to be sung in the temple itself, when the pilgrims have reached their goal. They range themselves alongside the servants of the Lord whose job it is to ensure his continuous praise, gliding off without limit into the night. For this reason, this prayer is often used in churches as a night prayer.

It is notable that in the first two verses 'you' is plural, while in the third it becomes singular. The pilgrims address the servants of the Lord in the plural, encouraging them to bless the Lord, but the Lord's own blessing is on the individual. So there are two different senses of blessing – the way we bless the Lord and the way the Lord blesses us. These are sometimes differentiated in translation by spelling: the Lord is 'blest', but human beings are 'blessed' by the Lord. The latter is simple enough to understand – at any rate, to a certain level. In the Old Testament, God blesses Israel with prosperity, often understood in terms of wealth and children. However, this is not always the case, for the challenge of the Beatitudes warns us that God's blessing does not always mean 'happiness' in the sense of fun and enjoyment. 'Happy those who mourn… who are persecuted… who hunger and thirst'? No! This makes no sense. It is rather that, despite appearances, the Lord's hand hovers over those who mourn, who are persecuted, who hunger and thirst. They are assured that they are in his safekeeping, despite their immediate strain and suffering.

More problematic is the former sense. How can we bless him who is forever blessed? How can we contribute anything to the Blessed One? Perhaps we can best make sense of the idea by joining it to praise and thanks. Thanks for a gift and praise for the giver often manifest themselves in making a fuss, showing the present around. This is the instinct that brings so many doxologies into the psalms, and especially the noisy and tumultuous trio of psalms with which the psalter ends, praising the Lord with the maximum number of noisy musical instruments. That is how we bless the Lord, whether it adds to the infinite divine glory or not.

Psalm 134[135]: Praise the name of the Lord!

This psalm has the classic form of a psalm of praise – an invitation to praise the Lord, followed by the reasons for praising (vv. 3–18), and finally returning to further encouragement to praise (v. 19). The reasons given in this case for praising the Lord are the choice of Israel and God's special care of his people (vv. 3-4), the universal creative power of God (vv. 5-7), the wonders of God at the exodus, leading Israel into the land of Canaan (vv. 8-12), and the vanity of idols (vv. 15-18).

Most of these themes occur frequently in the Bible, and it is widely suggested that this psalm is a late reflection, drawing on themes that were already familiar, and gathering texts from elsewhere. Much of it seems to be almost verbatim quotation of other biblical passages. Particularly close are verses 6-7, about God's creative power, and Jeremiah 10:12-13. Similarly, verses 10-12, about the conquest of the kings, are almost identical to Psalm 135[136]:18-21, but without the refrain. Finally, the mockery of idols in verses 15-18 is paralleled by several passages in the second part of Isaiah, notably Isaiah 44:9-20. It is difficult to fix the direction of borrowing by establishing the date of the psalm. But it is more likely that the single author of this psalm has assembled themes from three or more different biblical passages than that three or more authors independently used the same psalm as a quarry.

Our task is, however, to appreciate the psalm as it stands rather than to dig into its ancestry. For someone chronologically minded, it moves rather splendidly forwards. Starting with the divine splendour in the heavens, beside which no pagan gods have any standing (v. 5), it then reflects on divine power over the universe, shown in the power of the weather (vv. 6-7). Moving on to the history of Israel, it reflects on the manifestation of divine power in Egypt, during Israel's wanderings and at the time of the entry into Canaan (vv. 8-14). The last topic for praise is the contrast between the Lord and idols, a matter that preoccupied Israel during the exile (vv. 15-18). Borrowed or not, it makes a harmonious and progressive whole, enclosed within the initial and final exhortations to praise God.

Psalm 135[136]: For his love endures forever

On various occasions we have met psalms with a simple refrain, which may well have been repeated as a response to a soloist (for example, Psalms 23[24] and 45[46]). Now, the response runs right through the psalm. This acclamation about God's love (or mercy) appears as the response to a first line in several psalms – Psalms 105[106], 106[107] and 117[118] (in the first three verses) – and elsewhere. It might well have been used more widely than is currently attested, rather like *Kyrie, eleison* in the Greek Orthodox liturgy, which is used frequently and repeatedly as a response to almost any prayer. It is tempting to say that 'For his love endures forever' is the basic theme and cry of all Israel's liturgy.

As we have seen before, God's *hesed* is the unfailing, forgiving family love that God has for Israel. It is the cement of the whole nation, uniting them all. It is as a forgiving and loving God that the Lord is defined from his first self-identification on Sinai, constantly through the Bible, to Jonah and beyond. Any list of marginal references for Exodus 34:6 will show the overwhelming diffusion of this concept of God.

The matters announced and acclaimed match those of the previous psalm, but without the mockery of idols. There is more detail about the creation of the heavens and earth, seemingly dependent on the narrative of Genesis 1, where the sun and the moon – venerated as gods by many of the surrounding peoples – are plastered on to the heavens as mere timepieces.

With the help of the refrain, the whole psalm has become a rousing paean of praise to God's love for Israel. To the Gentile ear it rings a little oddly to sing, 'The firstborn of the Egyptians he smote' and 'Kings in their splendour he slew', and then add 'for his mercy endures forever'. What has happened to the kindness of God toward the firstborn of the Egyptians and the unfortunate Sihon and Og? The answer is, of course, that they fall outside the family love of God for Israel. There is no point in chiding Israel for its narrow nationalism. The promises to Abraham were for the sake of all nations, but it took centuries of the development of revelation for this truth to move from the back-burner to the front of Israel's consciousness.

Psalm 136[137]: By the rivers of Babylon

This song is perhaps both the saddest and the most brutal of all the songs of the psalter, bringing us vividly to the devastation of the exiles in Babylon. Their inability to sing a song of the Lord on alien soil is not simply a matter of brokenheartedness; it has also a theological basis. The story of Naaman makes clear that, during the period of the Israelite monarchy, it was still presumed that God was the God of Israel, and could be worshipped only there. One of the benefits of the searing experience of the exile was the realisation that the gods of the heathens were nothing, and that Yahweh was Lord of the whole earth.

So, at the beginning of the exile, the Judeans felt that they could not worship the Lord in Babylon. They were cut off from all that they had held most sacred. It was not simply that they were too upset to give their captors a little ethnic concert. They were cut off from the solace of prayer. This really is to be alone in the world, with only the longing for Jerusalem.

With all-too-human reaction, this sorrow boils over into a strident cry for revenge, an insistence far more positively ferocious than the mere neglect of Sihon and Og that we saw in the previous psalm. Edom was an old foe, its enmity expressed in the struggle between Jacob and Esau, named also Edom, and festering throughout Israelite history. The hostility of the prophets (Ezekiel 25:12–14 and especially Obadiah) shows that Edom had taken the opportunity to cash in on the devastation of Jerusalem by Nebuchadnezzar. The enmity engendered contributed to the resentment felt centuries later against the half-Edomite Herod the Great.

Before we self-righteously condemn the psalm's spirit of national vengeance, however, it might be well to remember the atrocities of Christian anti-Semitism and apartheid, not to mention the Christian toleration and use of slavery for so many centuries. We can remain blind, even before God, to the evil we have taken for granted for years. An appropriate prayer, sparked by the final verses of this psalm, might be that the Lord would stir our consciences and open our eyes to evil in our own midst.

Psalm 137[138]: I thank you, Lord, with all my heart

This psalm peaks with the glory of the Lord. It begins with the psalmist's blessings and gratitude to the Lord, mounting to include the gratitude of the great kings of the earth, and ending with a prayer of confidence in the Lord's care in any situation. But the point of focus is the glory of the Lord (v. 5). We have already considered this awesome, daunting and attractive quality – the glory of God, which was the most the people of Israel could bear to see of God in Exodus 34:30–30, and the vision that overwhelmed the prophet in Isaiah 6:1–5. The Christian, however, cannot fail to note that this glory was also to be seen in Jesus, the human and visible expression of God, and the symbol or sacrament of God's glory.

The Prologue to John's gospel puts it starkly and unmistakably. After describing the Word who was with God before all eternity, through whom all things were made, it concludes, 'We have seen his glory, the glory as of a father's only son' (John 1:14, NRSV). In the Bible, 'glory' is a specifically divine quality, which belongs to no one else, so already this puts Jesus on the level of God. At the first miracle, during the marriage feast at Cana, Jesus let his glory be seen (2:11).

The same is true, perhaps less explicitly but no less impressively, in the other gospels. In the early stories in Mark there is a mounting awe and wonder: first Jesus teaches with supreme authority, unlike the scribes (1:22). Then he has the audacity to forgive sins, which in itself constitutes a divine claim, as the onlookers indignantly object (2:5-6). Then he commands the wind and the sea as only God can (4:41; Psalm 106[107]:28-29). Then he comes walking on the water (Mark 6:48), and only God walks on the backs of the waves (Job 9:8). Further on, at the transfiguration (Mark 9:2-7), he is seen in heavenly glory, speaking with Moses and Elijah, who had themselves witnessed the glory of God on the holy mountain. No wonder Peter and the apostles were terrified and dumbfounded! Finally he is to come to judge the world 'in *his* glory' with *his* angels (and only God has angels), taking his seat on *his* throne of glory (Matthew 25:31).

We do indeed have cause to thank the Lord that we are protected by that glory, and that this glory became visible in Christ our Lord, the image of the unseen God.

Psalm 138[139]: O Lord, you search me and you know me

This gentle and loving psalm about God's care for the poet has many similarities with the book of Job, but at the same time it is so different in spirit that it could almost be a deliberate counterpoint to Job.

Job feels himself pursued by a hostile God who torments him and will give him no moment of relief so that he can 'swallow his spittle' (7:19). Yet paradoxically, at the same time Job clings to God as his only source of salvation. Our psalmist feels only one side of this – the tenderness of God's unremitting care, wherever he may be, moving up, down or to the side (vv. 8-9; compare Job 23:8-9). Unlike Job, he does not want to escape but rests in the security of God's ubiquitous presence.

There is the same appeal to Sheol, although for Job it is a place to hide from God's anger (Job 14:13), while for the psalmist it is the place where he is lovingly formed by God (vv. 11–13). The towering finale of Job grants the unapproachable omniscience of God (chs. 38—41), which confounds Job's protests. Our psalmist agrees that God's thoughts transcend human comprehension (vv. 6, 17), but for him it is a source of unalloyed comfort.

The motif running through this delicate psalm is friendship with God. The psalmist feels that he has been formed with infinite care and views his own creation as an affectionate, personal gift from the Creator. It is rather like a well-chosen birthday present: the recipient knows and appreciates the care that has gone into making or choosing the gift. God saw everything that would happen to the psalmist and planned his formation accordingly: 'every one of my days was decreed before one of them came into being' (v. 16). The instrument is perfectly fitted for the job. Yet there is no trace of arrogance in the psalmist's pleasure in what he is, for he really does attribute 'the wonder of his being' (v. 14) to God's careful formation. This is true humility, to delight in our talents and skills, realising that they are not of our own making but of God's.

Nevertheless, finally we are pulled up short by a little outburst of imprecation against the wicked (vv. 19–22). I find this much less strident than other such outbursts, for it appears as the result of the psalmist's friendship with God: he is protesting not on his own behalf but on God's, because the 'men of blood' rebel against God and interfere with God's designs.

Psalm 139[140]: The poison of viper on their lips

In this psalm, the title is verse 1.

The sentiment of 'an eye for an eye and a tooth for a tooth' dominates this prayer against enemies. It is not exactly the spirituality of turning the other cheek that Jesus taught, but it is worth remembering that 'an eye for an eye' was originally itself a limitation of vengeance: the injured person should not take vengeance beyond the extent of the injury suffered (Exodus 21:23–25). You can't break your attacker's arm when he has only scratched your skin.

Nevertheless, it is staggering to see how barely the teaching of Jesus has entered the Christian consciousness. On the rare occasions when a heroic mother or father forgives the killer (deliberate or not) of a child, it is greeted with cries of disbelief or even indignation. Yes, such a loss is almost inconceivably terrible, for the suffering makes a permanent wound and such forgiveness is indeed heroic, but it is only one of the heroisms to which the Christian has signed up. Perhaps forgiveness of little or great injuries is the hardest and most frequent of the ways in which we – created in the image of God – must imitate God. After the Lord's Prayer, in Matthew 6:14, mutual forgiveness is the one petition stressed by the addition 'If you forgive others their failings, your heavenly Father will forgive you yours.' In Matthew 18, on how we should behave to one another in community, half the chapter is devoted to forgiveness.

What of the Lord avenging 'the poor' and 'the needy' (v. 13)? I write in Africa, surrounded by poverty and need. A village boy has just come to borrow a hoe so that his mother can plant some melon seeds in the arid and dusty soil. Should we comfortable westerners not be trembling in our shoes as we purr towards the well-stocked shelves of the supermarket?

Meanwhile, we can also admire the neat structure of the psalm: verses 2–6 and 9–12 concentrate on the injuries suffered and threatened, interspersed with two quatrains (vv. 7–8 and 13, beginning 'I have said' and 'I know') attesting God's unfailing help. The injuries threatened by the attacker are also neatly paralleled by the psalmist's own threats: the poison of a viper on their lips (v. 4) is to be balanced by the malice of their speech overwhelming them (v. 10), and the hidden trap (v. 6) by being flung into the abyss (v. 11). These two hurtful actions are balanced again (in reverse order) by 'violence' and 'slander' in verse 12.

Psalm 140[141]: Lord, set a guard over my lips

A reflection of this kind has no business to present and discuss the views of scholars about textual ambiguities. A comparison of the almost laughably different translations of this psalm will show that the ancient Hebrew text of verses 6–7 is so hopelessly corrupt that it is difficult to make any sense at all of them. We shall not attempt to do so.

A main theme of the psalm is prayer, 'the raising of my hands like an evening oblation' (v. 2). It is a prayer to stay close to the Lord, to evade temptations and the allurements of evil company by keeping our eyes turned towards the Lord God. What is, then, the purpose of prayer? Is it to bend God's will to mine, to persuade God to change his mind? Nothing we do can change God's plan! It is a natural Christian instinct to voice our desires and needs to our Father in heaven, to share with God our worries and ambitions, as friends and families share theirs. But in prayer to God, this sharing always carries the implication of submission to and acceptance of the Father's good pleasure. Rather than moving God towards ourselves, we move ourselves towards God, coming closer to him and putting ourselves under the protection of his loving and fatherly benevolence. No matter how pressing our perceived need, no matter how passionate our longing, no matter how well-deserved the granting of our petition, the basic thrust of our prayer is to shelter under God's wings.

So in this psalm the fear is that we might fall in with the evil speech and actions of the wrongdoers. How easy it is to allow our conversation to take on a sneering or destructive tone from those around us, to cap one calumny with another, one lie with another! And how easy it is to fall in with the 'evil deeds' of 'men who are sinners' (v. 4) – the line of least resistance, the quick gain that others around us pursue, the evasion of the unpalatable duty! 'Everyone does it, so why shouldn't I?'

Apart from the unintelligible two verses in the middle of the psalm, it is a prayer that our loyalty to God and our trust in his care may keep us close enough and devoted enough to avoid 'the snares of those who do evil' (v. 9).

Psalm 141[142]: To the Lord I cry out with my plea

In this psalm, the title is verse 1.

This is a psalm of total desolation: 'Nobody cares whether I live or die' (v. 5). There is no strength in the psalmist himself and no help anywhere at hand, and yet somehow, by the end, he has confidence that the Lord will deliver him and there will be a joyful celebration with his friends for his liberty. It is impossible to determine the physical circumstances of this desperate plea, for all the concrete terms – such as a trap hidden in the path and release from prison – are often used metaphorically, just as enemies are often portrayed as raging bulls and fierce dogs in a single psalm.

In a way, the very vagueness of the situation is comforting: there is no situation so desperate in human terms that the Lord cannot be relied on to solve it. Of course, we cannot expect the Lord to wave a magic wand to wipe out our own folly or failure. The solution may be that God enables us to become reconciled to our situation in humility and perseverance. Failure and folly are great teachers: there was a wise old monk who used to talk about 'kick-things', stupidities for which you want to kick yourself when you think them over at night in bed. 'How *could* I have done that?'

If we have the little bit of strength needed to admit these stupidities, we may even share them with our friends for the amusement of everyone, including ourselves – when 'the upright gather round me' (v. 7). Together we learn that we are not so wise, so strong or so 'savvy' as we thought, and that God is always there after all to pick up the bits. He is 'watching over my path', if only 'in his presence I unfold my troubles' (vv. 3–4). The admission of failure is a powerful solace and a powerful start to rebuilding – and of course the Lord knows about those 'kick-things' anyway!

Psalm 142[143]: A sinner's hope

In a devotion of prayer, traditional since the seventh century, this is the last of the seven penitential psalms, to be prayed on any occasion of a deep repentance. The psalmist is well aware of his sin and the punishment that is due. The summing-up in verse 2, 'no one is just in your sight', forms the conclusion of Paul's great statement in Romans 3 that the whole world is sunk in sin and in need of redemption (vv. 10–20).

The situation is not hopeless, for the psalmist appeals twice each to those wonderful concepts, the saving justice (vv. 1, 11) and the faithful love (vv. 8, 12) of God. God's justice is not like human justice, founded on laws, the penalties of laws and the imposition of punishment where punishment is due. Of God's justice it is possible to say, as in Psalm 7:11, 'God is an upright judge, slow to anger': a human judge must be stern where sternness is due. Then we find, in Isaiah 46:13, 'I am bringing my justice nearer… my salvation will not delay' (compare Isaiah 51:6). Human justice is often a matter of condemnation, not of salvation. God's justice is a matter of fidelity, not to a code of laws of conduct but to his own promises of protecting Israel and all its members, the promises made repeatedly to Abraham, Isaac, Jacob and Moses. It is a promise to justify, in the sense of bringing back to true. A similar usage remains in modern printer's English: 'justifying a margin' means bringing the margin back to true instead of leaving jagged edges. So God's justice is a saving justice, on which Israel can rely.

Equally reliable is the concept of 'faithful love'. This has nothing to do with finding someone attractive or amusing, or their company enjoyable. It is the love that will never desert and never fail, the love of a mother who gets up in the night for her ailing or fractious child, or David's love for Absalom. Even after Absalom had rebelled against his father, thrust him out of Jerusalem and lain with his concubines in full sight of the sun, David's mourning for Absalom at his death could still drive the brutal and practical Joab to expostulate, 'I can see that you would be content if we were all dead, provided that Absalom was alive' (2 Samuel 19:7). Essentially it is love for the family, blood family or fictive family, and we are all God's family.

So, despite our sins, the saving justice and the faithful love of God still give us grounds for hope.

Psalm 143[144]: The blessings of victory and peace

The first ten verses of this psalm are largely adopted from other psalms, notably Psalm 17[18], with a dash of Psalms 8, 32[33] and 38[39]. The final verse of the psalm is a repeat of Psalm 32[33]:12.

It is not easy to see the cohesion between these borrowings, but, at any rate, those from Psalm 17[18] are a prayer for success in battle.

The first, warlike, part of Psalm 143[144] (vv. 1–10) can be read as an unusually diffident battle-prayer, recognising that there is no possibility of success without the Lord's help. It opens with a strong statement of the power of God and of the psalmist's reliance on God, and then sets the contrast with human frailty. In Psalm 8, human beings are regarded as the crown of creation, to whom the rest of creation is subject, but in this psalm the quotation of Psalm 8 leads into a very different and much less confident sentiment: 'Human life [is] a mere puff of wind' (v. 4). So the leader prays for divine intervention in the classic imagery of the storm-god of lightning and thunderbolt, derived from the imagery of Baal, the Canaanite storm-god.

The happy tone of verses 9–10 suggests that victory has been achieved, although the end of verse 10 still prays for deliverance from the sword of evil. The king is described as 'your servant David', as a reminder of the promises made to David in the Lord's name by the prophet Nathan in 2 Samuel 7: his dynasty shall last forever and his throne shall be secure forever. This may, of course, be the reason why the title 'Of David' was added to the psalm.

The last part of the psalm (vv. 12–14) is a gentle and attractive prayer for family and agricultural prosperity. If the two halves of the psalm are indeed to be understood as a unity, this picture of lasting peace, the overflowing blessing of the Lord, can be seen as a further stage after the achievement of the military victory prayed for in the earlier part of the psalm.

Psalm 144[145]: I shall praise you to the heights, God my King

We come now to the last of the acrostic psalms, those literary *tours de force* in which each verse begins with a consecutive letter of the alphabet. This seems to me a far stricter form and, therefore, a far greater achievement than any rhyming couplets such as we have in English. It also has the advantage of making it easier for the singer to remember the order in which the verses come – very useful if the poem is somewhat repetitive, as this one is. This psalm also has a neat 'envelope', the final verse more or less repeating the first verse.

Another exciting feature is that the verse beginning with the Hebrew letter *nun* (v. 13b) was missing in all versions – Hebrew and Greek and other translations – until it was discovered in the mid-20th century in one of the manuscripts hidden in the caves of Qumran. These manuscripts have contributed in all kinds of ways to our knowledge of the background of the foundation of the church. The case also poses an interesting question: should these newly discovered words now be slipped into the text that has always been considered inspired and formative for the Christian church? Most authorities give it the benefit of the doubt and include it in its due place between verses 13 and 14. After all, its theological contribution is not staggering or bewildering. But what if the lost letter of Paul to the Laodiceans (mentioned in Colossians 4:16) were found? And what if it disagreed with other teachings of Paul? Would it be included as 'inspired scripture' in the basic and normative teaching of Christianity?

The psalm is a joyful song of praise of the Lord and the divine generosity in all kinds of ways. The first ten verses concentrate on the necessity and the joy of praising the Lord. They are full of verbs such as 'praise', 'recount', 'proclaim', 'acclaim', 'speak' and 'bless'. The next ten verses concentrate more on the many diverse aspects that the psalmist wishes to praise: divine generosity, support and answer to prayer. In the centre, and perhaps as the climax, comes gratitude for the revelation of the kingship of the Lord (vv. 11–13). God's revelation of himself is indeed the greatest of all his gifts, a gift of himself in friendship, inviting us to a response in faith and friendship. Without this revelation of the nature of God, given in so many ways throughout the Bible, we would be dependent for our understanding of ourselves and our position in the world on natural philosophy – and that does not get us far. Knowing God as king, we have an anchor to our being and our place in the universe.

Psalm 145[146]: Praise the Lord, my soul!

We have come to the end of this group of eight psalms attributed to David, and we enter upon the final chorus of praise: each of the last five psalms of the Psalter begins with 'Alleluia', the Hebrew for 'Praise (*hallelu*) the Lord' (the sacred name YHWH, shortened to *Yah*). This psalm has two striking features.

First comes a slap in the face: there is no such thing as life after death (v. 4). This is a particularly stark statement. We must face the fact that revelation is a continuous process, and that belief in a future life with God, after our physical death, developed only gradually, although there are hints of it and longings for it in many biblical writings. These hints are particularly prominent in the Psalms; the Greek version, especially, makes much of them. There is an awareness that God can never desert his loved ones. However, the praise of God here, without any hope of life after death, shows that the objective of devotion to God is a permanent loving relationship in *this* life: 'I will praise the Lord all my life' (v. 2).

Correspondingly, the second valuable feature is the echo of Isaiah 35:5–7, 49:9 and 61:1–2 in verses 7–9 of our psalm, outlining the healing wonders that the Lord will perform at the hoped-for establishment of the kingdom – justice for the oppressed, food to the hungry, freedom for prisoners, sight to the blind. These not only echo Isaiah but also look forward to the wonders of Jesus. When the imprisoned John the Baptist sent messengers to Jesus, asking whether he really was the Messiah (for John the Baptist expected a Messiah of judgment, who would separate the wheat from the chaff and cast the chaff into the furnace), Jesus sent back the message that he was fulfilling precisely these promises of Isaiah (Matthew 11:2–6).

Finally, verse 5 of the psalm does not refer directly to Isaiah; rather, it is related to the whole principle of the Law given to Moses. If we wish to be members of God's holy people, we must behave towards the immigrant, the orphan and the widow as God behaved towards the Israelites when they were immigrants, orphans and widows in Egypt. These reminiscences of Isaiah and of the Law give us quite enough of a programme for our own task of spreading God's kingdom.

Psalm 146–147[147]: The wisdom of God in creation

At last we come to the end of the double numbering of the psalms. As explained in the Introduction, the Greek and Hebrew numbering differs from as early as Psalm 9, since the Hebrew splits the Greek Psalm 9 into two, Psalms 9 and 10. Now the process is reversed: the Greek Psalm 147 is composed of the two Hebrew Psalms 146 and 147.

The stress on the rebuilding of Jerusalem and the gathering of the exiles means that the psalm must be post-exilic. We can imagine it as the prayer of the beleaguered little community gathered round Jerusalem. It can conveniently be read in three sections, each beginning with an invocation to praise the Lord (vv. 1, 7, 12). Then follows a reason for praise of God's care of the universe: his naming each of the stars (v. 4), providing rain for agricultural growth (v. 8), and sending the winter phenomena of snow and frost (v. 16). Each section ends with a comment on God's care for human beings: he sustains the poor, his pleasure is in those who fear him, and he reveals his word to Jacob. His special care is for Israel.

Against this background of the ordered universe, in which each element has its place and purpose, it is important to recall that, to the Hebrew mind, God created the world by his wisdom (so verse 5). Appreciation for this wisdom is clear in the delight and delicacy with which the various weather phenomena are here described. The thought is greatly developed in the biblical Wisdom literature in the last centuries before Christ. In Proverbs 8:22–31, Wisdom herself proclaims that God 'created me, first-fruits of his fashioning, before the oldest of his works... I was beside the master craftsman, delighting him day after day, ever at play in his presence.' So, in every detail, creation is the manifestation of the Wisdom of God.

In the New Testament, such language is applied to Christ, the 'image of God' and the firstborn and principle of both creation and re-creation, through whom all things came into being and through whom all things go to God (Colossians 1:15–18). A similar image is God's creative and effective word ('by the words of the Lord his works come into being and all creation obeys his will', Ecclesiasticus 42:15, in the Apocrypha), an image used in this psalm (vv. 15, 18–19) which will also be used of Christ in the Prologue of John's gospel: 'The Word was with God... Through him all things came into being' (John 1:1, 3).

Psalm 148: Let them praise the name of the Lord

The Psalter ends with three final great songs of praise. This first one calls upon all creatures (except insects!) to praise the Lord. First (vv. 1–6) come those in the heavens, and then (vv. 7–14) those on the earth and in the sea. Each litany begins with the words, 'Praise the Lord from the heavens [or] earth', and sums up with a verse that begins, 'Let them praise the name of the Lord' (vv. 5, 13).

The Hebrew world is pictured as a flat plate, resting on pillars (we are not quite sure what these would rest on!) in the middle of a formless and frightening watery waste. The water is held back by God, who has spread a brass dome over the earth to hold back the waters above. Moderate amounts of water are allowed to enter from below in the form of springs, and through sluice-gates in the heavens above as rain. God has also fastened the sun, moon and stars as time-markers in the brass dome. This picture is drawn from the Mesopotamian worldview, shorn of many pagan elements and, instead, enriched by the Hebrew view of God.

The Bible contains other similar litanies calling upon all creatures to praise God, of which the most popular is perhaps the Song of the Three Young Men in the fiery furnace in the Greek version of Daniel 3:51–90 (absent from the Hebrew). The litany of the psalm builds up to two mentions of the transcendence of the name of the Lord.

The 'name' stands for the nature and power of the Lord. It includes the awesomeness of the Lord as it was seen in the great visions of Isaiah 6 and Ezekiel 1, an awesomeness before which human nature can only tremble and run to hide, 'in terror of the Lord, at the brilliance of his majesty, when he arises to make the earth quake' (Isaiah 2:10, 19, 21). But it also includes the loving forgiveness of God, revealed to Moses on Mount Sinai as his name (Exodus 34:6), and on countless other occasions, such as when he sews garments to spare Adam and Eve their shame (Genesis 3:21). Neither of these conceptions is tolerable without the other. Perhaps Augustine put the dual attitude to God best when he said, '*Ardeo et inhorresco*, clumsily translated, 'I burn with love, but I shrink away in fear.'

Psalm 149: A two-edged sword in the hand

This penultimate psalm of praise falls into two halves (vv. 1–4 and 5–9). The first section is a cheerful hymn of praise, with rejoicing, delight, dance and musical instruments. The second part is somewhat militaristic.

The indications are that this is a late psalm. The king in verse 2 is not a king of David's line, but is the Lord-king, parallel to 'the Maker of Israel'; so clearly the Israelite monarchy has come to an end. The spirituality of 'the humble' (v. 4) is also a late, post-exilic feature. The wretched situation of the returned exiles, huddled round Jerusalem, oppressed by hostile neighbours and constantly harried by invasion, led them to a spirituality of emptiness, humility and reliance on God alone: 'Seek the Lord, all you humble of the earth' (Zephaniah 2:3).

Furthermore, the name *hasidim* or 'pious' for the 'faithful' of Israel (vv. 1, 5, 9) is a late feature; the word is still used today for ultimately observant Jews.

The most striking indication, however, is the image of praising God with 'a two-edged sword in their hand' (v. 6). This transports us immediately to the stories of the rebuilders of Jerusalem, in the teeth of opposition from the squatters who had appropriated the land during the absence of the Jews in their 70 years of Babylonian exile, 'working with one hand and holding a spear in the other. Each builder had his sword strapped to his side as he built' (Nehemiah 4:11–12). It would also fit the protracted and bloody struggle against the Syrians throughout the middle of the second century BC, a ding-dong war, during the whole of which the Syrians maintained a hated fortified presence in the citadel of Jerusalem, overlooking the temple itself.

Both these backgrounds give a different aspect to the militaristic and triumphalist language of the latter part of the psalm. The returned exiles were fighting for their existence, for the very survival of the Jewish faith and way of life, in what might be deemed a holy war. This is a different situation from the *herem* or 'ban' of total destruction, of which we hear in the stories of Joshua and the entry into Canaan (Joshua 6:17). Vengeance is never pretty, but self-defence in a battle for survival is less intolerable. We cannot judge those of an earlier and rougher age by our own standards of practical conduct. We may praise the Lord for the survival of that thin stream of renewed Judaism.

Psalm 150: Praise God in his holy place

Each of the five books of the Psalms ends with a doxology, the last being naturally the most elaborate. It matters not that we know little about musical instruments of the time. This is obviously a noisy celebration. We might almost say that whole-hearted praise needs to be noisy. In our sophisticated society, we have learned to restrain the noise, but all the organ stops come out for the final celebration.

It is important to be aware that these psalms, which have become so central to the liturgy of the church, are only a part of the prayers of praise and supplication present in the Bible. We do not know why they were chosen to be included among these 150 Psalms, nor how they were preserved and celebrated. There is still a rich treasury of other deeply moving and instructive prayers in both Old and New Testaments, which may help us to grow in understanding of the ways in which God has offered us his friendship and helps us to respond to them.

BRF

Transforming
lives and communities

Christian growth and understanding of the Bible

Resourcing individuals, groups and leaders in churches for their own spiritual journey and for their ministry

Church outreach in the local community

Offering three programmes that churches are embracing to great effect as they seek to engage with their local communities and transform lives

Teaching Christianity in primary schools

Working with children and teachers to explore Christianity creatively and confidently

Children's and family ministry

Working with churches and families to explore Christianity creatively and bring the Bible alive

Visit **brf.org.uk** for more information on BRF's work

brf.org.uk